MY WILL BOOK

MICHAEL G. TRACHTMAN

with

Dirk M. Simpson

Sterling Publishing Co., Inc.
New York

A JOHN BOSWELL ASSOCIATES BOOK

This book is not a substitute for legal advice. It cannot anticipate all individual circumstances and it cannot cover all jurisdictional differences in laws and procedures. While it is designed to provide accurate and authoritative information in regard to the subject matter covered, the author, publisher, and seller disclaim all liability for damage or loss caused by use of or reliance upon this book, they make no warranties regarding its accuracy or completeness, and they specifically disclaim all implied warranties, including the implied warranty of merchantability or fitness for a particular purpose. If you have a legal problem, or if you desire more than this book provides, you should consult with a competent legal professional.

design Nan Jernigan

Library of Congress Cataloging-in-Publication Data Available

10 9 8 7 6 5 4 3 2 1

Published by Sterling Publishing Co., Inc.
387 Park Avenue South, New York, NY 10016

© 2007 by Sterling Publishing Co., Inc.
Distributed in Canada by Sterling Publishing c/o Canadian Manda Group,
165 Dufferin Street Toronto, Ontario, Canada M6K 3H6
Distributed in the United Kingdom by GMC Distribution Services
Castle Place, 166 High Street, Lewes, East Sussex, England BN7 1XU
Distributed in Australia by Capricorn Link (Australia) Pty. Ltd.
P.O. Box 704, Windsor, NSW 2756, Australia

Printed in China
All rights reserved

Sterling ISBN-13: 978-1-4027-4557-7
        ISBN-10: 1-4027-4557-5

For information about custom editions, special sales, premium and corporate purchases, please contact Sterling Special Sales Department at 800-805-5489 or specialsales@sterlingpub.com.

TABLE OF CONTENTS

ACKNOWLEDGMENTS

My colleagues in the Powell Trachtman law firm, Dirk M. Simpson and Jacklynn A. Barras, were invaluable in the preparation of this book. Dirk helped to develop and distill the advice, strategies, and forms in the book so that they would work across the country, and for the benefit of individuals and families in a wide variety of circumstances and living arrangements. This was a daunting task, and Dirk faced it relentlessly. As many times as I challenged Dirk with another of the problems this book seeks to address, he always found a practical, creative, and often unique solution. Dirk, in turn, depended on Jacklynn for additional research, analysis, and insight, and Jacklynn's contributions are evident through all aspects the book.

This book—a book that could not only explain a will, but could also *become* a will—was John Boswell's idea. John not only gave me the opportunity to write the book, he provided a wealth of insights and editorial solutions that helped us lose the "legalese" and make the book accessible and understandable. I am, as I have been many times in the past, most grateful.

Michael G. Trachtman

TO WHOM IT MAY CONCERN:
IN THE EVENT I DIE OR BECOME INCAPACITATED,
PLEASE FOLLOW THE INSTRUCTIONS SET FORTH BELOW

This book contains my will and my health-care power of attorney. I have prepared these documents for the purpose of helping my family and friends understand my intentions in the event of my death, or in the event I become incapacitated. My will provides clear instructions respecting the disposition of my assets upon my death. My health-care power of attorney provides clear instructions respecting what should be done in the event I become incapacitated.

My will names my executor, who is the person responsible for administering my will. My health-care power of attorney names my agent, who is the person I have authorized to make medical decisions on my behalf if I am not able to make those decisions for myself. In the event of my death, please notify my executor. In the event I am incapacitated, please notify my agent.

MY WILL

If I chose a short-form will, it is included within Chapter Four. If I chose a long-form will, it is included within Chapter Five.

My will does not include preprinted page numbers. Instead, so that there will be no confusion, I have hand-numbered each page of my will, and each of these page numbers states the total number of pages in my will.

You will find a signed witness statement and a signed self-proving affidavit in Chapter Six. These documents are also part of my will. They will make it easier to prove that this is, in fact, my genuine will.

All of the pages of my will are perforated so that they can be easily removed from this book when my will is probated. Upon my death, please remove all of the pages of my will from this book, including the witness statement and the self-proving affidavit, and fasten them together. You should then provide my will to my executor.

MY HEALTH-CARE POWER OF ATTORNEY

My health care power of attorney is included within Chapter Seven.

Like my will, each page is perforated so that it can be easily removed from this book. If I am incapacitated and unable to make health care decisions for myself, I ask that you remove my health-care power of attorney from this book, and fasten the pages together. You should then provide my health-care power of attorney to my agent.

CHAPTER ONE

The Goal: Peace of Mind for Yourself and Your Loved Ones

Whether you are single, married, or living in a so-called nontraditional relationship, whether you are divorced or widowed, whether you are just starting your career or have long since retired, whether you have no children, small children, or grown children, and no matter where in the United States you may live, you are holding in your hands some of the most important protections you can provide for yourself and your loved ones. Literally. By picking up this book you have taken the critical first step toward ensuring that you and your loved ones won't be saddled with the tragic uncertainties that so often arise should you suffer a debilitating illness or injury, or die without having done the appropriate planning.

Here is how it works. By following the simple steps and instructions in the following chapters, this book will itself *become* two of the most important legal documents you will ever sign:

◆ Your will, through which you will state what you choose to do with your assets upon your death;

◆ Your health-care power of attorney which, like a living will, will help you take care of the medical and end-of-life decisions that will have to be made if you are unable to make these decisions for yourself.

Importantly, both of these documents are "portable"—they are designed to comply with every state's requirements. You won't have to worry about whether your will is enforceable if you move from New Jersey to Florida to California to the District of Columbia.

We've made it easy and inexpensive for you. And for no extra charge, we've thrown in the remarkable peace of mind that comes with knowing that you've gained control over a monumentally important aspect of your life.

WHY DO I NEED A WILL?

Surprisingly, approximately three out of every four Americans die without a will. Many put it off because they'd rather not contemplate their own mortality. Many think it's too expensive. Many think only rich people need wills. Many don't know how to begin the process. Many simply procrastinate.

But virtually all Americans who die without a will have this in common: they are shortchanging themselves and their loved ones.

Using this book, you can easily create a basic will that does what you won't be around to do.

◆ You can leave your property to the people and organizations you choose. Otherwise, the law of the state in which you live when you die will split up your property among your family members in accordance with a predefined ratio—whether or not that's what you would have preferred. Do you want to leave a special ring or painting to a friend or nephew? Do you want to make sure that your children and your elderly parents are properly provided for? Do you want to

1

keep a spouse from whom you are separated or a child from whom you are estranged from inheriting your assets? Do you want to support a particular charity? If so, you'd better have a will.

◆ Imagine the complications that will arise if both you and your spouse pass away in an accident. Unless you have a will, a judge will decide who will raise your children and how your assets will be spent for their benefit, without any input from you.

◆ Without a will, once your children turn eighteen they can spend whatever money or property they inherit from you on trips and cars, despite your hope that they would spend it on their college educations. Do you want to maintain some tighter controls? Do you want to create a simple trust to manage the money for the purposes you would prefer? If so, you'd better have a will.

◆ If you are in a nontraditional relationship and want your partner to inherit your assets, you'll need a will.

◆ You can name a trusted person as your executor—the person with authority to make sure that the terms of your will are carried out and that sensible decisions are made. Lots of unforeseen issues and disputes can arise after you are gone, and you will want to make sure that a person you can trust is in charge. To do that, you will need a will.

WHY DO I NEED A HEALTH-CARE POWER OF ATTORNEY?

Here's another of life's unpleasant possibilities: you may suffer an accident or an illness that leaves you unable to make crucial health-care decisions for yourself, even including decisions involving the choice between life and death. Is it fair to leave those decisions to your spouse, parents, or children, without any authority or guidance? Suppose they disagree?

A health-care power of attorney provides a workable solution. This book will provide you with the ability to create one that is simple, clear, and effective.

IS THIS BOOK FOR ME?

This book is designed for all kinds of persons and all kinds of families. It includes a short-form will option for people who have simple and uncomplicated estate-planning needs. It also includes a long-form will option for people who need more alternatives and flexibility. We will explain which choice is right for you later in the book.

At the same time, this book is not for everyone. Some people need the services of an attorney who specializes in estate-planning, and you should most definitely check with an attorney if you have any doubts. Nevertheless, even in situations best suited for estate-planning experts, this book will provide you with a great head start at organizing your thoughts and intentions, and getting a handle on the decisions you will need to make.

Here are some of the more common situations in which an estate-planning attorney should be consulted.

◆ Federal estate taxes can be triggered if you own more than $2 million in assets (including, for instance, the value of your business and face value of your life insurance policies). Anything less than that is presently exempt from federal estate taxes. So if your assets are in or above that neighborhood, you'll need some professional tax-planning strategies.[1]

---

1. Under the law as it now exists, this threshold is to be increased to $3.5 million in 2009; the entire federal estate tax is to be repealed in 2010; and it is then scheduled to come back in 2011 with only a $1 million exemption. However, the chatter among congressional observers is that the federal estate-tax laws will be revised prior to 2010, perhaps with a $5 million permanent exemption.

◆ In most states your will could be vulnerable to a challenge by your spouse if you leave your spouse less than a certain percentage of your assets. (Remember that your spouse is still your spouse, even if you have been separated for decades, until you are legally divorced.) The number varies by state, but a safe rule of thumb is 50 percent. If you want to leave your spouse less than 50 percent of your assets, and you think your spouse might challenge your will because of that decision, you should get some help from a qualified attorney.

◆ If you have a child, parent, or other loved one who requires long-term support and medical assistance from government programs, you should consult an estate-planning attorney. Money or property left to people who need such help may disqualify them from government assistance.

◆ If you own and operate a business, you may need some help to properly plan how to deal with your business after you are gone. If, for instance, you choose to leave everything to your spouse and/or children you'll need to determine if they have the ability and desire to work in the business, or whether you should instead implement a mechanism to turn the business into cash. Estate-planning lawyers deal with these situations all the time.

GETTING STARTED

The goal of this book is to help you complete your will and your health-care power of attorney forms so that they are legally enforceable no matter where in the United States you may choose to live, and so that they effectively implement your intentions and preferences.

Three logistical cautions before we begin:

1. DO NOT SIGN YOUR WILL UNTIL YOU HAVE READ CHAPTER SIX.

In order to assure its validity, your will must be signed in front of witnesses and a notary public, in compliance with certain legal procedures, as explained in Chapter Six.

2. MAKE COPIES OF THE BLANK FORMS BEFORE YOU FILL THEM IN.

As your circumstances change over the years, you may want to revise your will and your health-care power of attorney. Don't do this by making changes to a form you have already completed. If a court sees erasures, cross-outs, or alterations, it may conclude that the form was changed after you died or became incapacitated, and your will or health care power of attorney could be invalidated. Instead, make a photocopy of each of the forms before you begin to fill them in, and store the photocopy of the blank forms in this book for future reference. If you want to make changes to any form, use the blank photocopy—but before you do so, make another photocopy so you always have at least one blank form in reserve. To avoid confusion, destroy the old version of any form you have filled in as soon as you complete a new version.

3. LEAVE YOUR COMPLETED WILL AND HEALTH-CARE POWER OF ATTORNEY FORMS IN THIS BOOK.

For safekeeping, leave all of the pages in this book. The "To Whom It May Concern" instruction at the beginning of the book tells your survivors how to remove the pages that comprise your will and your health-care power of attorney and properly assemble them.

CHAPTER TWO

What You Can—and Can't—Give Away in Your Will

As a general rule, when you write your will, you can give away whatever you own at the time of your death to whomever you want. But there is an important exception to this rule: like many people, you may own certain items of property that will, at the instant you die, automatically become the property of someone else. As a result, these items of property cannot be passed on through your will. Any provisions in your will that attempt to give away these items of property will be ignored, after it's too late for you to do anything about it.

It can be easy to forget or misconstrue which, if any, items of your property will be treated in this way when you die. A mistake won't invalidate the rest of your will, but it could end up negating your plans and intentions, and creating disappointment and confusion in those you intended to remember in your will.

Consequently, it's worth spending some time to distinguish what you can and can't give away in your will.

FOUR RED FLAGS: HOW YOU CAN TELL THE DIFFERENCE BETWEEN WHAT YOU CAN AND CAN'T GIVE AWAY IN YOUR WILL

For most people, distinguishing what you can and can't give away in your will won't be a difficult task—there are "red flags" that will clearly warn you of potential issues. Yes, there will be exceptions and unusual situations and, as always, if you have any doubts or questions you should consult with a professional. But in the majority of instances, the red flags will be quite obvious.

You will use what you learn in this chapter to complete two asset inventory worksheets in the next chapter—one to compile a list of what you can give away in your will, and another to compile a list of what you can't give away in your will. Once the worksheets are completed, you'll then be set to begin the process of writing your will. As an added bonus, the worksheets will be an invaluable resource for your family and your executor as they try to understand, locate, and manage your property after your death.

Red Flag #1
PROPERTY JOINTLY OWNED BY A HUSBAND AND A WIFE
Perhaps the most commonly misunderstood context in which these potential problems arise involves property that is jointly owned by a husband and a wife. It seems counterintuitive but, depending on the circumstances, you might not be able to give away your share of the property you own jointly with your spouse at the time of your death.

This anomaly has its roots in the old English laws that our founding fathers brought with them when they colonized the Americas. According to those laws, a husband and a wife were viewed not as separate persons, but as an indivisible husband-wife entity. Consequently, when the husband and wife acquired property in their joint names during their marriage, the law mandated that the property was owned by the husband-wife entity, not by the husband and wife as individuals. In effect, during their marriage, the husband and wife each owned all of their joint property, as opposed to each of them owning half of their property.

This way of looking at joint property owned by married couples had some important practical consequences. For instance, since both spouses owned all of their joint property, neither spouse could transfer, mortgage, or otherwise dispose of any part of their joint property without the consent of the other spouse. The law effectively mandated that all financial decisions had to be joint decisions.

And, most important for our purposes, neither spouse could give away any part of their joint property in their will. Instead, because they both owned the whole of each item of their joint property, at the instant one of them passed away, the other became the sole owner of the property, automatically, by operation of law. If, for instance, a husband wrote a will leaving his share of some jointly owned land or jewelry to a poor relative or a charity, that provision of his will would be viewed as an invalid attempt to give away what he did not own.

Surprisingly, these medieval notions of marriage and property remain in effect to varying degrees in many states throughout the country and, as a result, you'll need to be careful if you wish to write a will that gives away property you own jointly with your spouse at the time of your death.

There are two things you should look for and think about in order to determine if these rules will apply to you. The United States remains a crazy quilt of state-specific laws, and it is virtually impossible to set forth general propositions that apply everywhere, all the time. But the following approach will work in the vast majority of cases.

ALERT: **Once a husband and a wife are officially divorced, these arcane rules no longer apply. At that time, the husband and wife become subject to the same rules as normally apply to other joint owners of property—absent an agreement to the contrary, each of them can do what they want with their share of what they own. But keep in mind that the divorce has to be final for this change in status to take effect. Even if you've been separated for ten years, and even if divorce proceedings are pending, you're still married in the eyes of the law.**

First: check the ownership documents. The old English concept of the way in which a husband and a wife own their joint property is called a "tenancy by the entireties," and the husband and wife are referred to as "tenants by the entireties." Property owned in this way is referred to as "entireties property." These terms are the law's equivalent of magic words, and you should look at the documents that pertain to the title of the property to see if any of these terms appear. If they do, it is very likely that you won't be able to give away any of this property in your will.

"Real estate" (sometimes called "real property") is the legal term for land and the buildings and other structures attached to land. If you own a building lot, a house, a condo, or an investment in an apartment building, you own real estate. There will always be a deed or other document that reflects how real estate is owned. When a married couple acquires real estate, title clerks or attorneys will frequently insert the magic words (for instance, something like "Joe Jones and Sally Jones, husband and wife, as tenants by the entireties") without the husband's or wife's knowledge or consent. Be sure to check for this language.

"Personal property" is the legal term for every other kind of property—cars, bank accounts, furniture, stock certificates, jewelry, intellectual property (such as patents, copyrights, and trademarks), animals, and so on. Not all personal property comes with documents reflecting ownership. But the most valuable personal property owned by many married couples—their savings and investment accounts—do come with ownership documents, and personnel at financial institutions such as banks and brokerage houses often use the "tenants by entireties" terminology as a matter of course when setting up these accounts. Again, look for the magic words.

Second: check the state where you lived when you and your spouse acquired the property. About half of the states have laws mandating the following: if you and your spouse jointly acquire property in one of these states, that property will be deemed to be owned by the two of you as tenants by the entireties, even if your deed or other ownership documents do not include the "tenancy by the entireties" magic words. In these states, the law foists this type of ownership arrangement on married couples, whether they want it or not.

The following states have laws of this type—note that in the states marked with an asterisk, the law applies only to real estate, not personal property: Alaska*, Arkansas, Delaware, District of Columbia, Florida, Hawaii (only if there is clear proof of the intent to create a tenancy by the entireties), Illinois*, Indiana*, Kentucky*, Maryland, Massachusetts (only if there is clear proof of the intent to create a tenancy by the entireties), Michigan, Mississippi, Missouri, New Jersey, New York*, North Carolina*, Ohio* (the rule only applies to real estate obtained before April 4, 1985), Oklahoma, Oregon*, Pennsylvania, Rhode Island, Tennessee, Vermont, Virginia, and Wyoming.

Generally, these laws will only apply if the husband and wife simultaneously acquire a joint interest in the property during their marriage. If, for instance, you and your fiancé close on a house the day before you get married, the house probably won't become entireties property after the wedding ceremony. If you buy some stock in your individual name and later put it into joint name with your spouse, it's unlikely that you will be forced into a tenancy by the entireties.

Note, however, that once your joint property is rightly deemed to be entireties property under one state's law, it will remain entireties property even if you and your spouse relocate to another state that has a contrary law.

ALERT: **If you live in a "community property" state, an additional rule applies. Community property states include Alaska, Arizona, California, Idaho, Louisiana, Nevada, New Mexico, Texas, Washington, and Wisconsin. In these states, any property either spouse obtains in his or her individual name during the marriage is deemed to be community property. This means that, by law, each spouse owns half of the property acquired by the other spouse during the marriage, even if the property is not in joint names, and was never intended to be owned by both spouses. This has a very significant effect on the will-drafting process. There are some differences from state to state, but as a general proposition if you live in a community property state, and if you obtain property in your individual name while you are married, you can only give half of it away in your will.**

You can change all this business about tenants by the entireties and community property by way of an agreement with your spouse, such as a prenuptial or postnuptial agreement. But beware—these kinds of agreements must conform to strict legal standards or they won't be enforceable. You'll definitely need a lawyer.

Red Flag #2
PROPERTY OWNED WITH A "RIGHT OF SURVIVORSHIP"

If you jointly own real estate or personal property with one or more other persons aside from your spouse, there's another set of magic words to look for in the deed and other ownership documents that pertain to the property: "right of survivorship." If you see that phrase, chances are you won't be able to give that property away in your will.

Joint property owners who have a "right of survivorship" are treated much like spouses who own property as tenants by the entireties: when a fellow joint owner passes away, the surviving joint owner(s) immediately get the deceased joint owner's interest in the property, without having to pay for it. In situations where, for instance, there are five joint owners with a right of survivorship, and one of them dies, his or her interest will instantly pass to the others in accordance with their proportionate ownership interests.

For will-drafting purposes, the upshot is this: if you jointly own property in which your fellow owners have a right of survivorship, you will have no ownership interest in that property to pass on to your heirs when you die—whatever you owned will belong to the other joint owners.

In order for jointly owned property to be owned with a right of survivorship, the joint owners must all agree on that arrangement in advance—unlike a tenancy by the entireties, this form of ownership can't be imposed on you by operation of law. In addition, the "right of survivorship" phrase, or something close to it, must be in the deed or other ownership documents that pertain to the property. You'll see a phrase something like "Joe Jones and Sally Smith, joint owners with a right of survivorship" in the documents. Often, the phrase "joint tenants with a right of survivorship" is used, and you will frequently see this abbreviated as "JTWROS."

Keep the other side of this coin in mind. If there is no tenancy by the entireties or right of survivorship, and so long as the joint owners have not made some other agreement, each joint owner of real estate or personal property can do what they want with what they own, including giving it away in their will.

Red Flag #3
BUSINESS BUY-SELL AGREEMENTS

Business partners, if well advised, will usually enter into something called a "buy-sell agreement." If you own an interest in a business and signed this type of agreement, you won't be able to pass on your interest in the business through your will.

Business buy-sell agreements serve an important function. Here's how they work.

Suppose that you and two partners start a business. You form a corporation and you each own one-third of the stock. You and your partners trust and complement one another and, over time, the business thrives, it buys a building and equipment, and your stock becomes your most valuable asset.

Now suppose that one of your partners dies, and in his will he left all of his assets to his son—an eighteen-year-old with neither expertise nor ambition who is suddenly entitled to one-third of the profits. Or suppose that you die first, having left all of your assets to your wife. She will now have to figure out how to protect her interest in a business with which she is unfamiliar, while dealing with two partners who don't want to deal with her.

Literally overnight, many businesses have been transformed from thriving to troubled enterprises, and many families have been thrown into tumult, as the result of such situations.

Buy-sell agreements were invented to prevent these kinds of scenarios. A buy-sell agreement provides that upon a business owner's death, the remaining owners are required to buy the deceased owner's interest in the business for a predetermined, fair price (often book value, or a price derived from a formula). The deceased owner won't be able to pass on his interest in the business to his heirs, but he will be able to pass on the cash that will be paid to his estate in exchange for his interest in the business. If handled correctly, this creates a win-win for all concerned: the remaining owners know that the deceased owner's interest in the business won't fall into the hands of someone they might not want as a colleague, and the deceased owner's heirs will get fair value for the business interest they would have inherited.

If you own an interest in a business, confirm whether you and the other owners signed a buy-sell agreement before you begin planning on how to dispose of your business interest in your will. And if you and the other owners did not sign a buy-sell agreement, you should consult with a lawyer and seriously consider whether it would be in the best interests of yourself and your heirs to do so.

Red Flag #4
PROPERTY WITH A NAMED BENEFICIARY
If you own a life insurance policy, you designated a beneficiary to receive the death benefit upon your death. Obviously, you cannot write a will that will leave that death benefit to someone else.

Most people understand that this is the way it works with life insurance, but they sometimes forget that they may have also designated beneficiaries for other types of property. The possibility that you named beneficiaries to receive your other property upon your death is a red flag that you should investigate when you write your will.

For example, when you filled out the paperwork for your 401(k), IRA, or other retirement plan, you may have been asked to choose a beneficiary to whom the money in the plan will go on your death. Many people forget that their retirement plan is set up in this way, and in their wills they try to leave the money in the plan to someone else. Check the paperwork, or call the plan administrator.

You may also have a financial account in which you designated a named beneficiary to receive the balance in the account upon your death. These accounts are sometimes referred to as "POD" (for "pay on death"), or "TOD" (for "transfer on death"). Sometimes they are referred to as "Totten trust" or "informal trust" accounts. Similar arrangements often apply to certain types of annuities and other investment arrangements. Check the paperwork and, if necessary, contact the institution that holds the account.

WHAT'S "PROBATE" AND HOW WILL IT AFFECT YOU?

As a matter of proper legal terminology, the property you can give away through your will is often referred to as "probate property," and the property you cannot give away through your will is often referred to as "non-probate property." This is because after your death, the property that you give away through your will is handled through a legal procedure called "probate."

Many people have heard the term "probate" and have come to believe that it is something they should avoid, without really knowing what it is.

"Probate" is a legal procedure designed to protect you, not hurt you. It refers to the legal process through which a will is administered. By "probating" a will, you invoke the authority of a neutral third party—the local court—to make sure that the "probate property" described in the will goes where it is supposed to go, and that everyone who is interested in the will is treated fairly.

This can be important. There's always the possibility that an executor will play favorites among the beneficiaries, or will charge too much, or will fail to carry out the intentions of the person who wrote the will. The probate process is intended to give the beneficiaries the peace of mind that comes from knowing that a neutral authority is holding everyone accountable so that no one gets taken advantage of.

For most persons who use the will forms in this book, probate will be a fairly routine and non-intimidating procedure. After your death, someone (usually a family member, friend, or attorney) will present your will to a clerk in the courthouse office responsible for initiating the probate process (usually a person in the Register of Wills department). The clerk will want to see if the will has been properly signed and witnessed—something we cover in Chapter Six. Once that hurdle is cleared, the clerk will issue documents that grant the executor named in the will the legal authority required to carry out the terms of the will. After the executor has completed these tasks, the court will then invoke certain procedures designed to make sure that the will was administered in accordance with the intentions of the person who wrote it, that the beneficiaries were treated fairly, and that the assets in the estate were properly handled.

Still, probate has earned a bad name, sometimes deservedly, because of the filing fees and delays involved in the process. Probate fees are usually based on the value of the probate property, and can vary tremendously by state. There may also be various add-on charges.

Generally speaking, however, for people with probate property valued at under $2 million, average probate fees will probably range from $200 to $1,500. Simple estates average only a few hundred dollars in probate fees, and can normally be wrapped up in a few months. For those kinds of estates, which are most of the estates appropriate for this book's will forms, the concern over the probate process is usually unjustified, and the advantages will outweigh the disadvantages.

Many people take pains to convert the property they would normally give away in their will into property that automatically goes where they want it go when they die—using the legal terminology, they convert their probate property into non-probate property that passes outside of their will.

You can, for instance, convert your bank accounts and investments into joint accounts with a right of survivorship so that a loved one will automatically own them when you die. This can be a good thing, so long as you work it all into your overall planning process. You don't pay any probate fees or incur any probate delays on nonprobate property. And, in most cases, your general creditors at the time of your death (that is, the people and companies who don't already have a mortgage or lien on your property) won't be able to get their hands on nonprobate property. They can only recover against the assets in your estate.

But it's not always quite so simple.

The amount of probate fees you save by going to this trouble may not be worth it, and depending on exactly how you do it, by putting your property into the form of nonprobate property you may lose valuable rights to the property that you might not be able to get back should your circumstances or intentions change. That can have disastrous consequences.

Some people play fast and loose with these techniques. For instance, they might change the title to property without really giving away any rights, and that can have all kinds of unintended consequences—stashing shares of stock in your child's name but taking the dividends for yourself, for example, might be very interesting to the IRS unless it is handled in precisely the right way.

Some people figure they can avoid probate and defeat their creditors merely by putting their assets in someone else's name before they die. Wrong. Virtually all states have laws prohibiting "fraudulent conveyances"—that is, property transfers made without getting fair value in return that leave you or your estate without the assets to satisfy creditors. A creditor can go to court and reverse a fraudulent conveyance.

To pursue these kinds of strategies the right way, you'll need competent legal counsel.

ALERT: **There is a common myth that avoiding probate will help you avoid federal estate taxes. It's not so. If your estate is at or above the minimum federal estate-tax threshold, currently $2 million, you may have a tax liability whether or not you avoid probate. As mentioned earlier, if your estate is in this ballpark, you should be consulting with an estate planning attorney.**

ALERT: **So-called living trust forms have been mass-marketed as devices that will help to avoid probate. They may well, but for many people the cost of the living trust will exceed the probate fees they would otherwise incur. And many people assume that these arrangements will allow them to avoid federal estate taxes or creditor claims—it is just not so.**

A FINAL WORD FOR MARRIED COUPLES

If you are married (or if you think you may get married in the future), there's one more thing you should know.

As mentioned in the previous chapter, most states have laws that require you to leave a certain percentage of your estate to your spouse. The percentage varies from state to state, but 50 percent is fairly common. If your will does not satisfy this requirement, your surviving spouse may have the right to take from your estate the mandatory share provided by the law, no matter what your will says. Your surviving spouse will have this right so long as you are legally married at the time of your death, even if you have been separated for many years.

For most married couple, this won't be a problem. Most married couples choose to leave the bulk of their estates to their spouses, or they take care of their spouses through nonprobate property (such as life insurance) and leave most of what they have to their children. In other situations, couples usually work out the details before their death and agree on the best way to handle things. In those instances, the likelihood of your spouse challenging your will after your death are minimal, and it's probably not worth worrying about any of this.

If you do wish to leave your spouse less than half of your estate and you think there is a risk that your spouse will challenge your will on that basis, you should see an estate-planning lawyer. Sometimes you can resolve this through a prenuptial, postnuptial, or other agreement, but these arrangements are tricky, and you'll definitely need the assistance of counsel.

CHAPTER THREE

Your Asset Inventory Worksheets

Writing a will is, fundamentally, a two-step process. First, you will need to list what you own so that you will know what you will be giving away. Second, you will need to decide who gets what. This chapter focuses on the first step, and will help you inventory your assets in a way that will make the second step much easier.

The process of making a list of your assets sounds simple, and in many cases it is. Still, until you actually sit down and focus on the task, it can be easy to overlook or underestimate what you have. At the same time, you don't have to list every lamp, sofa, lawn mower, and coffee pot. You should list the items that have significant monetary value, and you should list the items that are important to you for sentimental or other reasons. These are things that you might want to earmark in your will for a specific person. Everything else can be lumped together in categories, such as furniture, garden equipment, kitchen equipment, and so on.

As you know from the last chapter, you may own property that you can't give away in your will. Because of this, it makes sense to create two lists as you go through this process—one list for property you can give away in your will, and another list for property you can't give away in your will. For this purpose, we have created two asset inventory worksheets that you'll see immediately below. The worksheets also include a space to insert to whom (or to what) you want to give the property you can give away, and who is going to get the property you can't give away.

Listing your assets in this way offers a variety of benefits. Once you create a "can give away" list you'll be able to plainly see what you've got to work with and what decisions you'll have to make when you write your will. Once you create a "can't give away" list you'll know who's getting taken care of through the nonprobate property that passes outside of your will, and that might influence your choice on what you'd like to do with the probate property that you will be giving away through your will. To make it easier for you, we have partially filled in these forms with some of the most commonly owned types of property that fit into the "can give away" and "can't give away" categories, but don't stop there. As you decide which item of property belongs on which list, think about the four red flags from Chapter Two.

It won't be the end of the world if you don't get this absolutely right. Your will won't be invalid just because you made a mistake. But the better you do, the less confusion you will create, and the more likely it will be that things will turn out as you intended.

LISTING THE PROPERTY YOU CAN GIVE AWAY UNDER YOUR WILL

Use Asset Inventory Worksheet #1, which follows, to list the property you *can* give away under your will.

Remember that if you own something jointly with one or more other persons (and it is not entireties property or subject to a right of survivorship) you should only list the value of your share on this worksheet. For instance if you and a friend jointly own an investment property, include only the value of your half of the property on this form.

Note that the last column on the form asks for the "net value" of the asset—this means what the asset is worth, less any debt that is owed on that asset. This will show you the real value of what you're giving away so you can make sure that this squares with your intent. If you own a vacation condo that is worth $200,000 and you have a $75,000 balance on your mortgage, the net value is $125,000. If you own a car that is worth $10,000, but you still owe $2,000 on the car loan, the net value is $8,000. If you and your two siblings jointly own an investment property (and the deed says nothing about a right of survivorship), then you own a one-third share that you can give away in your will. If the property has a fair market value of $400,000 and a $100,000 mortgage debt, then you would subtract the debt from the value of the property to obtain the net value of the property ($300,000). The value of what you own would be your share of the property times its net value: 1/3 x $300,000 = $100,000.

Note also that at the very end of the worksheet you are to state the amount of your general claims and debts, and subtract that from the total value of property on this list. When we talk about general claims and debts we mean the sums you owe others that are not tied to a particular item of property, like your house mortgage or your car loan (which you would have already listed on the form)—for example, credit-card debt, school loans, and so on.

This is the only way you'll be able to get a true picture of what you are really giving away in your will. For instance, if you die with an unpaid credit-card debt, the credit-card company will probably be entitled to be paid first, even if that means taking shares of stock or selling some other item or property you designated for a particular heir.

If you have a lot of creditors, you may be tempted to give away as much of your assets as you can afford before you die, in the effort to keep those assets out of the reach of creditors after you die. However, remember what was said in Chapter Two about fraudulent conveyances—it is not that easy and, in particular, deathbed asset transfers that are obviously intended to cheat creditors will not stand up. If you're worried about how much of your estate will be eaten up by creditors, you should consult with an estate-planning attorney.

One final word. We listed the value of any business interest you may own on this "can give away" worksheet, whether or not it is subject to a buy-sell agreement. If there is no buy-sell agreement, list the net value of your interest in the business; if there is a buy-sell agreement, list the amount of cash your estate will receive for your business interest as mandated by the buy-sell agreement.

LISTING THE PROPERTY YOU CAN'T GIVE AWAY UNDER YOUR WILL

Use Asset Inventory Worksheet #2 to list the property you *can't* give away under your will—your nonprobate property.

As with Asset Inventory Worksheet #1, list the "net value" of each item so you'll know what it's really worth. For instance, there may be a mortgage against property you own as tenants by the entireties or with a right of survivorship, or you may have taken out a loan against your 401(k).

ASSET INVENTORY WORKSHEET #1
Property You Can Give Away Under Your Will

Identify the Asset	Who Do You Want to Give This to Under Your Will?	What Is the Net Value (Value Less Any Debt)?
Checking Account		
Savings Account		
Stocks/Bonds/Mutual Funds		
Cash/Money Market Account		
Residence		
Other Real Estate (Vacation Home, Time Shares, Rental Properties, etc.)		
Value of Business Interest (or cash payment owing if subject to a buy-sell)		
Valuable Jewelry Item		
Valuable Jewelry Item		
Valuable Jewelry Item		
Valuable Jewelry Item		
Other Jewelry		

Identify the Asset	Who Do You Want to Give This to Under Your Will?	What Is the Net Value (Value Less Any Debt)?
Valuable Art, Antiques, Furnishings Item		
Valuable Art, Antiques, Furnishings Item		
Valuable Art, Antiques, Furnishings Item		
Other Art, Antiques, Furnishings Item		
Clothing		
Household and Garden Items		
Vehicles		
Computers and Other Electronic Equipment		
Total Value		
General Claims and Debts		
Total Value Less General Claims and Debts		

ASSET INVENTORY WORKSHEET #2
Property You Can't Give Away Under Your Will

Identify the Asset	Who Gets It Upon Your Death	What Is the Net Value (Value Less Any Debt)?
401(k) with a Designated Beneficiary		
IRA with a Designated Beneficiary		
Other Pension Plan with a Designated Beneficiary		
Profit-Sharing Plan/Stock Options with a Designated Beneficiary		
Transfer on Death (TOD) and Payable on Death (POD) Accounts with a Designated Beneficiary		
Other Financial Instruments/Accounts with a Designated Beneficiary		
Life Insurance		
Real Estate Owned as Tenants by the Entireties		
Real Estate Owned as Tenants by the Entireties		

Identify the Asset	Who Gets It Upon Your Death	What Is the Net Value (Value Less Any Debt)?
Other Property Owned as Tenants by the Entireties		
Other Property Owned as Tenants by the Entireties		
Real Estate Owned with a Right of Survivorship		
Real Estate Owned with a Right of Survivorship		
Other Property Owned with a Right of Survivorship		
Other Property Owned with a Right of Survivorship		
Total Value		

CHAPTER FOUR

The Short Form

Now that you have a handle on the property you can give away through your will and the property that your heirs will inherit outside of your will, you can begin the process of actually writing your will.

Some people need no more than a very structured and simple will form. For those people, this chapter includes a short-form will. Others need a will form that includes some additional options. For those people, we have provided a long-form will in Chapter Five. The next section of this chapter will help you decide which form is best for you.

No matter which will form you choose, the process of writing your will works in the same way. Both this chapter and the next chapter are divided into several sections, each corresponding to a part of your will. Within each section is an explanation that tells you what that particular part of your will is all about and how to complete it. You will then fill in the blanks of that part of your will. The end result will be a completed will, ready for signature.

REMEMBER THE THREE POINTS STRESSED AT THE END OF CHAPTER ONE. *First*, don't sign your will until you have read Chapter Six. To be effective, your will has to be signed in front of witnesses and a notary public. *Second*, make an extra copy of each of the blank forms and store them in this book before you begin. Never make erasures, cross-outs, or similar changes to your will once it's completed. Instead, when you need to make a change, use a blank form. *Third*, leave the completed forms in the book for safekeeping. The "To Whom It May

Concern" notice in the front of the book instructs your survivors on what they should do with the forms upon your death.

SHOULD I USE THE SHORT-FORM WILL OR THE LONG-FORM WILL?

The short-form will provides a very structured approach that meets the needs of many, but not all people. Here's what will happen to your assets if you use the short-form will.

- If you have a spouse with whom you are living or a designated domestic partner when you die, everything you have will go to him or her.
- If you don't have a spouse with whom you are living or a designated domestic partner when you die, everything will go to your children (or, in the case of any child who predeceases you, to that child's children).
- If you have neither a spouse with whom you are living, nor a designated domestic partner, nor any children or grandchildren when you die, everything you have will go the beneficiaries you name in your will.

If, instead of using this approach, you want to divide up your assets in a different way, such as giving particular items of property to other individuals or organizations, use the long-form will.

In addition, it's a good idea to use the long-form will if you are going to leave assets to young children (or even young adults). You obviously would not want to leave a substantial amount of money or property to a four-year-old child, and you might even want to control how an eighteen-year-old child (or, for that matter, a twenty-five-year-old child) is allowed to handle the money or property you leave him or her in your will. The long-form will provides you with some ways to handle these kinds of situations, including the appointment of a guardian and the creation of a "young person's trust."

WRITING YOUR SHORT-FORM WILL

The short-form will begins immediately after this section. Page through the short-form will now, before you begin filling in the blanks in the form, so you will have a feel for what it includes and how it works.

Identification Section. You will obviously need to identify yourself. Use the name you customarily use when you sign official documents, such as your application for your driver's license, your tax returns, or your bank account forms. If you have ever used a different name and continue to own property in that name, identify yourself by both names: "Matthew Gooding, also known as Matthew Good." You should also state where you reside, which can have legal importance.

Will Section 1: Revocation. This is standard language that revokes and cancels any previous wills that you may have made. This helps to prevent confusion over the validity of your current will. A revocation clause is appropriate regardless of whether or not you have made a prior will. You do not need to add or delete any language in this section.

Will Section 2: Status. Place your initials next to the appropriate sentence, designating whether you are married, unmarried, or in a so-called non-traditional relationship. If you are married, write your spouse's full legal name in the blank. Note

that if you are unmarried when you create your will and later die married, the short-form will automatically adjusts and provides that everything goes to your spouse (as defined in Will Section 7, explained below) at the time of your death.

If you are living in a nontraditional relationship with someone to whom you are not married, you can, if you choose, designate that person as your "partner," and under the short-form will he or she will then inherit all of your assets upon your death. Use your partner's full legal name. If your relationship changes, it will be very important to revise your will accordingly—otherwise, the partner you name will inherit your estate even though your relationship may have terminated.

Will Section 3: Residuary Estate. This section provides that your property will be distributed as follows.

◆ *If you die married or in a non traditional relationship,* your spouse (as defined in Will Section 7, explained below) or, if applicable, your named partner will inherit your entire estate.

◆ *If you die without a spouse or named partner, and had children during your life*, your children (as defined in Will Section 7, explained below) will inherit your estate in equal shares. If one or more of your children dies before you do, that child's children (your grandchildren) will inherit your deceased child's portion in equal shares, and if your deceased child leaves no living children, your other living children will inherit the deceased child's portion, in equal shares. As mentioned previously, if this provision might result in a young child inheriting money or property, consider using the long-form will.

◆ *If you die without a spouse or partner and have no children or offspring of children who survive you*, then you will have to name one or more alternate beneficiaries. You can, for instance make your beneficiaries your parents, or your best friends, or an organization such as a charity or a school. Unless you specifically designate percentages (such as "30 percent to Paul Logan, 70 percent to Bruce Lombardo") your beneficiaries will inherit equal shares of your estate. Remember that if you are using percentages they must add up to 100 percent.

Note that if you choose to leave some or all of your assets to a particular person, and if you want only that person to receive the assets if he or she survives you (that is, you don't want the assets to go to the person's descendants), phrase it this way: "Mark Cornish, but only if he survives me." In this example, if Mark Cornish predeceases you, his share will pass equally to your other beneficiaries and not to his heirs.

If, however, you want whatever you leave to that person to go to his or her descendants if he or she dies before you do, phrase it this way: "Sandra Mannix, or if she does not survive me, to her descendants, per stirpes." This means that if your chosen beneficiary is not alive when you die, that beneficiary's descendants will take his or her share in equal proportions. The term "per stirpes" is legal language that literally means "per branch." The effect is to divide what you left to a deceased person equally among that person's descendants.

Here's an example. Suppose that you have a son and two daughters. Your son has two children of his own. You write a will leaving your assets to your children, per stirpes. Your son passes away before you do. By using the "per stirpes" language, your son's one-third share will be split among his children (that is, your grandchildren will each receive one-sixth of your estate) and your two daughters will each receive a one-third share. Without the "per stirpes" language, each one of your children and grandchildren would receive an equal share.

Will Section 4: Choosing Your Executor. This section of your will requires that you choose who will serve as executor of your estate. The executor's job is to collect and preserve all estate assets, pay all appropriate debts, expenses, and taxes, and distribute the remainder according to the terms of your will. You are free to select just about anyone to serve as your executor. Here are a few pointers.

◆ In most simple and uncomplicated estates, it is usually best to appoint a trusted family member or friend (as opposed to an attorney, an accountant, a bank, or a trust company). Even if your executor is not experienced in such matters, he or she will retain an attorney or other professionals as needed. The most important requirement is that you choose an executor who can be trusted to act promptly and fairly according to the terms of your will.

◆ If you think the administration of your estate could occasion a family feud, then an outsider may make sense. This may be, but need not be, a professional, like an attorney or an accountant, although this will increase the cost of estate administration. Banks and trust companies are generally not the best choice for modest estates because they can be impersonal and expensive.

◆ Executors are entitled to "reasonable compensation" for the services they render. The exact amount varies by state. Some state laws say only that payment must be reasonable in relation to the quality and extent of services provided, while other states establish a fee schedule with rates ranging, for example, from 5 percent of the first $100,000 of assets and phasing down to 1 percent thereafter. The will forms in this book are silent on the subject of fees. This will allow your executor to claim a fee in the amount permitted by state law. You can provide for a different fee, or that your executor serve without a fee (in which case you risk getting what you pay for). Should you wish to go that route, there is a blank at the end of the form entitled "Other Instructions" in which you could state, for instance: *"My Executor shall serve without compensation,"* or *"My Executor shall be paid no more than 2 percent of the value of my probate assets,"* or whatever else may be your preference.

◆ Since the executor you select may decline to serve, or be unable to serve, you should always appoint an alternate executor. There is a designated space in the form for this purpose.

◆ If possible, your executor should reside in the state where you live when you die. Some states won't allow non resident executors, or if they do they may require that they post a bond (even if your will says otherwise).

You will see that the executor clause in this Section gives your executor broad powers to carry out the terms of your will. There is nothing to add or change here. It is generally a bad idea to restrict these broad powers. executors need some flexibility.

Will Section 5: Survival Clause. Consider a situation where a husband and wife write wills in which they leave everything to each other, and in which they further provide that if the other spouse is already deceased, all of their assets go to their children from their respective prior marriages. Now suppose that the husband and wife are in a car accident, and the husband dies instantly, but the wife survives for a few days. In this scenario, the husband's estate will pass to the wife, and a few days later, when the wife dies, everything the husband had will end up with the wife's children from her prior marriage—the husband's children from his prior marriage will be shut out.

To protect against this scenario, your will includes a clause providing that the beneficiary to whom you leave your estate (spouse, partner or anyone else) must live more than sixty days longer

than you do in order to inherit what you leave them in your will.

Will Section 6: Construction. This explains that the term "testator" and "executor" as used in your will are meant to refer to either gender or both, singular and plural. This is a standard drafting provision that helps to prevent ambiguities.

Will Section 7: Definitions. This is a standard definitional clause. It defines your "spouse" as the person you have identified in Section 2 or, if you have not filled in that blank, the person to whom you are legally married at the time of your death. If, however, you are separated from that person at the time of your death, your will provides that your spouse shall be treated as having predeceased you—in other words, if you are separated, your spouse won't automatically inherit your entire estate.

This definition anticipates the fact that many separated spouses enter into written agreements defining and limiting their respective property rights against one another, and you would not want a provision in your will that runs counter to this agreement. Note, however, that if you are separated and have not entered into such an agreement, your estranged spouse may have the right to challenge your short-form will since, as mentioned previously, for so long as you are legally married your spouse is entitled to a defined share of your assets, usually in the neighborhood of 50 percent, upon your death. If haven't made arrangements to satisfy this obligation (for instance, through non-probate assets or other arrangements) and you don't want to run that risk, you should use the long-form will.

This section also defines your "children" to include all natural born and adopted children that exist at the time of your death (including children born after you write your Will). As a result of this definition, when you leave property to your "children" under the short-form will, all of those covered by this definition will benefit, but your stepchildren will receive nothing. If you want to leave anything to your stepchildren, or if you wish to disinherit any of your "children," use the long-form will.

Will Section 8: Severability. This is standard protective language providing that if any part of your will is declared invalid, illegal, or inoperative for any reason, the remainder of your will survives.

Will Section 9: Optional Provisions. This section gives you the opportunity to state your preference regarding your burial or cremation. You don't have to fill in this section, and it's not legally binding but, hopefully, your survivors will respect your wishes. You simply need to initial your choice.

Will Section 10: Signature Line. **DON'T SIGN YOUR WILL YET.** You must sign your will in conformance with strict requirements involving the presence of witnesses and a notary public. All of this is explained in Chapter Six.

LAST TESTAMENT AND WILL

Last Testament and Will of _____

I, _____ a resident with an address of _____

_____, declare that this is my Will.

1. Revocation. I revoke all Wills that I have previously made.

2. Status. I have placed my initials next to the provisions below that I adopt as part of this Will. Any unmarked provision is not adopted by me and is not a part of this Will.

_____ I am not married at the time of making this Will. If I subsequently legally marry, but fail to update this Will to name my spouse, then I intend that my spouse be considered my "Spouse" for purposes of this Will.

_____ I am married to the following person who shall be considered my "Spouse" for purposes of this Will: _____.

_____ I am in a nontraditional relationship with the following person: _____ who, if designated, shall be referred to as my "Partner" for purposes of this Will.

3. Residue. Depending on my circumstances existing at the time of my death, I desire the following:

A. I give, devise, and bequeath all the rest, residue, and remainder of my estate, of whatever kind and wherever located, that I own at my death to my Spouse or Partner, as the case may be, if he or she survives me;

B. If I have no beneficiary under subsection 3(A) above, and I had Children during my lifetime, then I leave my residuary estate, in equal shares, to my Children, per stirpes;

C. If I have no beneficiary under either subsection 3(A) or 3(B) above, then I leave my residuary estate to the beneficiary(ies) I name below:

_____

_____

_____

_____

_____

Your initials*: _____
Witness #1 initials: _____
Witness #2 initials: _____
Witness #3 initials: _____
*sign your full name in Louisiana   Page _____ of _____

Any Bequests made in this Will to two or more beneficiaries shall be shared equally, unless a contrary intention is specifically indicated. I direct my Executor to sell all shared gifts and distribute the net proceeds as my Will directs, unless the beneficiaries of a particular gift unanimously agree in writing to my Executor that the gift shall be retained in kind.

If I name two or more beneficiaries to receive a bequest and one does not survive me, then, except as otherwise specifically provided, all surviving beneficiaries shall equally share the deceased primary beneficiaries' share.

4. Executor. I name _____ as Executor, to serve without bond or other surety. If the aforementioned person does not qualify, or ceases to serve, I name _____ as my alternate Executor, also to serve without bond or other surety.

I grant that my Executor take all actions legally permissible to probate this Will. These powers shall include all actions as my Executor deems to be in the best interests of my estate which shall include, but not be limited to, the following:

(A) To employ accountants, attorneys, investment counsel, agents, banks, or trust companies (collectively, "Professionals") to perform services for and at the expense of my estate. My Executor is expressly relieved of any liability or responsibility whatsoever for any act or failure to act by, or for following the advice of, any Professionals so long as my Executor exercises due care in their selection. Any compensation paid pursuant to this subparagraph shall not affect in any manner the amount of or the right of my Executor to receive compensation as my fiduciary.

(B) To retain any real or personal property, without liability for loss or depreciation resulting from such retention.

(C) To sell, exchange, or lease for any period of time, any real or personal property.

(D) To purchase all forms of property, including but not limited to stocks, bonds, notes and other securities, real estate, or any variety of real or personal property, without being confined to so-called legal investments and without regard for the principle of diversification.

Your initials*: _____
Witness #1 initials: _____
Witness #2 initials: _____
Witness #3 initials: _____
*sign your full name in Louisiana   Page _____ of _____

(E) To deal with and settle claims in favor of or against my estate without order of court.

(F) To vote stock; to convert bonds, notes, stocks, or other securities belonging to my estate into other securities; and to exercise all other rights and privileges of a person owning similar property.

(G) To continue, maintain, operate, or participate in any business which is a part of my estate, and to incorporate, dissolve, or otherwise change the form of organization of the business.

(H) To pay all debts and taxes that may be assessed against my estate, as provided under state law.

(I) To do all other acts which in my Executor's judgment may be necessary for the proper and advantageous management, investment, and distribution of my estate.

Other instructions:

_____

_____

_____

5. Survival Clause. If any beneficiary of this Will, including my Spouse or Partner, if any, shall die within sixty days of my death, I hereby declare that I shall be deemed to have survived such person.

6. Construction. As used herein, the terms "Testator" and "Executor" are meant to refer to either gender or both, singular and plural.

7. Definitions.
 A. "Spouse" shall mean the person named as my Spouse in section 2, or if not so named, the person to whom I am legally married at the time of my death; provided, however, if my Spouse is divorced from me or living separate from me at time of my death, my Spouse shall be treated as if he or she predeceased me.

B. "Children" shall refer to all my natural born or legally adopted children, whether now or hereafter born or adopted. "Children" shall not include stepchildren unless legally adopted.

Your initials*: _____
Witness #1 initials: _____
Witness #2 initials: _____
Witness #3 initials: _____
*sign your full name in Louisiana   Page _____ of _____

8. Severability. If any part of this Will is declared invalid, illegal, or inoperative for any reason, it is my intent that the remaining parts shall be effective and fully operative, and that any Court so interpreting this Will and any provision in it construe in favor of survival.

9. Optional Provisions. I have placed my initials next to the provisions below that I adopt as part of this Will. Any unmarked provision is not adopted by me and is not a part of this Will.

_____ I desire to be buried in the _____ cemetery located

at _____.

_____ I direct that my remains be cremated and that the ashes be disposed of according to the wishes of my Executor.

_____ I direct that my remains be cremated and that the ashes be disposed of in the following manner: _____

_____

10. Signature Line. I subscribe my name to this Will this ____ day of _____, _____, at _____, State of _____, and declare it is my last Will, that I sign it willingly, that I execute it as my free and voluntary act for the purposes expressed, and that I am of the age of majority or otherwise legally empowered to make a Will and under no constraint or undue influence.

_____
(Sign above)

Your initials*: _____
Witness #1 initials: _____
Witness #2 initials: _____
Witness #3 initials: _____
*sign your full name in Louisiana   Page _____ of _____

CHAPTER FIVE

The Long Form

This chapter includes the long-form will. Reread the Should I Use the Long-Form Will or the Short-Form Will section in Chapter Four—this will help you decide if the long-form will is right for you.

WRITING YOUR LONG-FORM WILL

Many of the provisions of the long-form will are identical to the coordinate provisions in the short-form will. Please refer to the designated sections in Chapter Four as indicated.

Identification Section. See Chapter Four.

Will Section 1: Revocation. See Chapter Four.

Will Section 2: Status. Define your status in this section. For example, if you are unmarried, write "I am single" in the blank. If you are married, write "I am married to [insert your spouse's full legal name]." For unmarried couples wishing to acknowledge their partner in a nontraditional relationship, write, "My Partner is [insert your partner's full legal name]."

Will Section 3: Identification of Children and Grandchildren. List all your natural born and adopted children and grandchildren who are alive at the time you sign your will. Under the long-form will, you don't have to leave anything to all, or any, of your children and grandchildren, but by listing them you will establish that you did not inadvertently overlook anyone. This can help to avoid family disputes after you pass away.

Note that the definition of "children" and "grandchildren" in this section includes all of your natural born and adopted children who are living at the time of your death (that is, even those born after you wrote your will), so if you do choose to give a gift to "my children" or "my grandchildren," they will all be included. Stepchildren, however, are not considered to be your "children" under the law. You must specifically list them in this section if you want them to be included as "children" under your will.

Now turn the page to complete sections 1, 2, and 3 of your will.

LAST TESTAMENT AND WILL

LAST TESTAMENT AND WILL OF _____

I, _____ a resident with an address of _____

_____, declare that this is my Will.

1. Revocation. I revoke all Wills that I have previously made.

2. Marital Status. _____.

3. Identification of Children and Grandchildren. I have the following children and grandchildren, all living when this Will was written and executed:

Children

_____

_____

_____

_____

_____

Grandchildren

_____

_____

_____

_____

The terms "my children" and "my grandchildren" include the aforementioned persons and include all children and grandchildren born after the making of this Will, and all children adopted by me. If I do not leave property to one or more of the children or grandchildren whom I have identified above, my failure to do so is intentional.

Your initials*: _____
Witness #1 initials: _____
Witness #2 initials: _____
Witness #3 initials: _____
*sign your full name in Louisiana   Page _____ of _____

Will Section 4: Bequests. This section of your will allows you to give away specific items of property. You can, for instance, give away property of purely sentimental value, such as family photos or mementos, or highly prized property such as artwork, jewelry, cash, or real estate. Before you complete this section, there are a few rules to keep in mind.[2]

◆ **Bequests Are Not Required.** You are not required to make any specific bequests. Instead, if you simply want to leave everything to one or more people (whether in equal shares or not), then you should skip to *Will Section 5: Residue Clause.* However, if you decide against making bequests, then you should write the word *"None"* in the blank so that there is no confusion about your intentions.

◆ **Bequests Take Priority.** Bequests are fulfilled prior to distribution of the remainder of your estate, which is called the "residue" of your estate. For this reason, it is not advisable to make substantial bequests which may risk leaving less than was originally intended for the persons to whom you left the residue of your estate.

For instance, suppose you have $300,000 in assets, mostly comprised of an interest in a business. You decide to make a bequest of $100,000 to charity, and you provide that the residue of your estate goes to your two children. However, by the time of your death many years later, you suffer some reversals, and your business is at that time worth only $10,000. If you failed to update your will, your executor will have the legal duty to pay $100,000 to charity, even if that means selling off the rest of your assets and leaving nothing for your children.

◆ **Bequests to Minors.** Giving items of substantial value to minors (such as your children) may create some complications. If you give money or property worth more than a certain amount to a minor (usually $2,500 to $5,000, depending on the state) you will have to name a property guardian to manage the money or property (and to periodically report to the local court) until the minor reaches the age of majority (anywhere from eighteen to twenty-one, depending on the state). The long-form will allows you to appoint a property guardian, as explained later in this chapter. However, when the minor reaches the age of majority, he or she will be given unrestricted access to this inheritance, regardless of maturity level. You can avoid that problem by setting up a simple young person's trust for your child, which is also explained later.

◆ **Be Specific.** Put yourself in the shoes of your executor and give him or her what is needed to carry out your intentions. If you make a bequest of "the diamond necklace my mother gave me" you'd better be sure that everyone knows what necklace you were referring to. It would be much better to make a bequest of "my necklace with the three round diamonds in the front and the gold chain."

◆ **Specify What Happens If Your Beneficiary Predeceases You.** You should name one or more primary beneficiaries for each bequest, and you should specify what happens if no primary beneficiary survives you. One option is to name one or more alternate beneficiaries in the space provided in the form. Another option is to state that if no primary beneficiary survives you, the bequest goes "to my residue." As noted above, this means that it will go into the pool of assets that is left over

---

2. Technically, if real estate is given away in a will, it is called a "devise." If other kinds of property is given away in a will (money, artwork, jewelry, and so on), it is called a "bequest." The term "legacy" is sometimes used interchangeably with the term "bequest," although it is properly used to describe a gift of cash. To keep things simple, this book generally refers to the act of giving property of any type away as a "bequest."

after all bequests have been distributed. How you should deal with your "residue" is explained in *Will Section 5*, later in this chapter.

◆ **Dealing with Mortgages, Liens, and Security Interests.** Your beneficiary will receive real estate subject to whatever mortgage remains on the property. Similarly, your beneficiary will receive other property subject to any existing security interest (for example, if you buy a diamond ring on an installment plan, the store may retain a security interest in the ring until the debt is fully paid). However, this general rule can be overridden by specifically providing that you are leaving the property free and clear of such debt. You can do this by including the following wording after each item you want to pass on in this way: "which shall pass free and clear of all debt, including mortgages, trust deeds, liens, and any other encumbrances."

For instance, if you want to leave your vacation home in North Carolina to Benjamin Taber free and clear of the mortgage, and if he does not survive you to the "residue" of your estate (explained below), here is how section 4 of your will should read:

4. Bequests. I make the following gifts of property:

I leave
<u>My vacation home located in Topsail Beach, North Carolina, together with all furnishings and possessions in the home, which shall pass free and clear of all debt, including mortgages, trust deeds, liens, and any other encumbrances</u> to <u>Benjamin Taber</u> _____
or, if such beneficiary(ies) do(es) not survive me, to <u>my Residue</u>_____.

But beware. This language does not cancel the debt; it merely changes the source from which the debt must be paid. If you leave a house with a $100,000 mortgage to your beneficiary "free and clear of all debt," your executor will then have to find the money in your estate to pay off the mortgage. That might not leave enough to satisfy your other bequests or intentions. Use your asset inventory worksheets, and update them from time to time, so you can make sure that there's enough to go around.

◆ **Shared Ownership.** Be careful about leaving items of property to more than one person. For example, consider the potential complications if you leave a house to your son and his wife. If your son ever gets divorced, do you want his former wife to be able to force a sale of the house and take half the proceeds? Or suppose you leave a valuable item of jewelry or artwork to your two children. That's a recipe for a family fight. To minimize those possibilities, this will empowers your executor to sell shared property and distribute the cash proceeds, unless the beneficiaries agree otherwise.

Also, this will includes language at the end of section 4 which states that shared gifts will be divided into equal shares, unless specified otherwise. Therefore, a gift of $10,000 to "Loretta and Amy" would pass $5,000 to each unless you state differently—for instance, "to Loretta (75 percent) and Amy (25 percent)." If you want Loretta and Amy to each get $10,000, then separately list each bequest on different lines. The language in the form also ensures that, in the absence of a contrary indication, a deceased beneficiary's share of a shared gift will be given to the surviving beneficiary or beneficiaries. Therefore, your bequest of $10,000 to Loretta and Amy will be given solely to Amy if Loretta has died before your executor finalizes the bequest.

◆ **Remember the Rights of Your Spouse.** As discussed previously, most states mandate that your spouse (that is, the person to whom you remain legally married, even if you are separated) receive a certain minimum percentage of your estate. If you violate these laws, your spouse could force your executor to give him or her the mandatory minimum, which could throw the rest of your will out of kilter. A good rule of thumb is to leave at least 50 percent of the net value of your combined probate and nonprobate assets to your spouse—unless you and your spouse have entered into a valid prenuptial agreement, postnuptial agreement, separation agreement, or other agreement that says otherwise (for which you will need legal counsel).

To comply with this requirement you should periodically update your asset inventory worksheets. When you first write your will, the total of the nonprobate and probate assets earmarked for your spouse might exceed 50 percent of all that you have. But as time goes on the nature and value of your assets may change, and the assets you planned to leave to your spouse may no longer satisfy the 50 percent target.

◆ **Homestead Rights.** If you own an interest in a home where you live with a spouse and/or minor children and you plan on making a bequest of your interest in the home to someone other than your spouse and/or minor children, be careful. Even if you've cleared the tenancy by the entireties and community property hurdles (see Chapter Two), some states have enacted "homestead laws" that will outlaw this bequest. These laws vary from state to state, but they basically mandate that upon your death, your spouse and/or minor children get the family home, no matter what your will says. You will be able to find out if you live in a state that has enacted a homestead law, and the details of that law, from your state's website, from your congressman, or at your local courthouse.

Now turn the page and complete section 4 of your will.

4. Bequests. I make the following gifts of property:

I leave _____

to _____

or, if such beneficiary(ies) do(es) not survive me, to _____.

I leave _____

to _____

or, if such beneficiary(ies) do(es) not survive me, to _____.

I leave _____

to _____

or, if such beneficiary(ies) do(es) not survive me, to _____.

I leave _____

to _____

or, if such beneficiary(ies) do(es) not survive me, to _____.

Any Bequests made in this Will to two or more beneficiaries shall be shared equally, unless a contrary intention is specifically indicated. I direct my Executor to sell all shared gifts and distribute the net proceeds as my Will directs, unless the beneficiaries of a particular gift unanimously agree in writing to my Executor that the gift shall be retained in kind.

If I name two or more primary beneficiaries to receive a bequest and one does not survive me, then, except as otherwise specifically provided, all surviving primary beneficiaries shall equally share the deceased primary beneficiaries' share.

If I name two or more alternate beneficiaries to receive a bequest and one does not survive me, then, except as otherwise specifically provided, all surviving alternate beneficiaries shall equally share the deceased alternate beneficiaries' share.

Your initials*:   _____
Witness #1 initials: _____
Witness #2 initials: _____
Witness #3 initials: _____
*sign your full name in Louisiana   Page _____ of _____

Will Section 5: Residue Clause. This is a very critical section of your will. It allows you to give away the "residue" of your estate—that is, everything that remains in your estate after payment of your debts and whatever bequests you chose to make. For many people, this will be the bulk of their estate. You should name one or more primary beneficiaries and one or more alternate beneficiaries in the spaces provided. As with your bequests, your residue will be shared equally among the beneficiaries entitled to the inheritance unless you state otherwise.

Also as with your bequests, if one of the beneficiaries dies before the residue is distributed, that beneficiary's share will be distributed to the other beneficiaries who are entitled to the residue. If you wish, however, you can instead pass the deceased beneficiary's share of the residue to his or her children and grandchildren. If this is your preference, use the legal language we discussed in Chapter Four: "or their lineal descendants, per stirpes." For instance, to accomplish this result you would fill in the blank in the will form as follows: "to my nephew and nieces, Edward, Melissa, and Amy, or their lineal descendants, per stirpes." If Edward dies before the Residue is distributed, his one-third share will go to his children (in equal shares), rather than to Melissa and Amy.

Now turn the page to complete section 5 of your will.

5. Residue Estate. I give, devise, and bequeath all the rest, residue, and remainder of my estate,

of whatever kind and wherever located, that I own at my death to: _____

_____

or, if such primary residue beneficiary(ies) do(es) not survive me, to _____

_____.

Any residuary gift made in this Will to two or more beneficiaries shall be shared equally, unless a contrary intention is specifically indicated. I direct my Executor to sell all shared gifts and distribute the net proceeds as my Will directs, unless the beneficiaries of a particular gift unanimously agree in writing to my Executor that the gift shall be retained in kind.

If I name two or more primary beneficiaries to receive a bequest and one does not survive me, then, except as otherwise specifically provided, all surviving primary beneficiaries shall equally share the deceased primary beneficiaries' share.

If I name two or more alternate beneficiaries to receive a bequest and one does not survive me, then, except as otherwise specifically provided, all surviving alternate beneficiaries shall equally share the deceased alternate beneficiaries' share.

Your initials*:   _____
Witness #1 initials: _____
Witness #2 initials: _____
Witness #3 initials: _____
*sign your full name in Louisiana   Page _____ of _____

Will Section 6: Choosing Your Executor. You'll need to carefully choose the people who will be responsible for carrying out the directives in your will. The first person you'll need to select is your executor. Refer to the instructions for choosing an executor in Chapter Four.

Will Section 7: Appointing Guardians for Minor Children. In addition to choosing an executor, parents of minors should also name a personal guardian to care for their children, and a property guardian to manage whatever money or other property is given to their children.

As for the personal guardian, if you have a spouse and you both want the other to serve as personal guardian if they survive you, you should both write wills naming the other, and naming the same alternate personal guardian. This will avoid confusion in case, for instance, you die at the same time.

Complications sometimes arise in the case of parents who are divorced or separated. Usually, a court will award custody to a surviving parent, but you can state in your will why the surviving parent is unfit in the effort to provoke a hearing in which a judge decides what's best for the child. Make sure your statements are provable and pertinent: a documented history of substance abuse, existing mental illness, or a criminal record may be important; the fact that the surviving parent was unfaithful may not be.

A court always has the right to override your choice of a personal guardian based on the child's best interests, so pick someone who will stand up to scrutiny. Be careful about naming a married or unmarried couple—you may create potential problems down the road if the couple splits up. The form in this book allows you to name only one personal guardian and one alternate for this reason.

As for a property guardian, as mentioned previously, if you leave more than a relatively small amount of money or property ($2,500 to $5,000, depending on the state) to a minor child, you will be required to appoint someone to manage the money or property until the minor reaches the age of majority. The surviving parent will typically serve as property guardian, but it is not automatic. If you want this to occur, say so, and if you prefer someone else, say why. A property guardian should be at least nineteen years old, and it is almost always best to name just one property guardian and one alternate for all your minor children.

In many instances, you will want to name the same person as personal guardian, property guardian, and the trustee of any young person's trust you establish under your will (explained later). This is entirely appropriate, and is a matter of personal choice.

If you don't have minor children at the time you make your will, write "not applicable" in the blanks on the form. This will prove that you failed to fill in these provisions on purpose.

Now turn the page and complete sections 6 and 7 of your will.

6. Executor. I name _____ as Executor, to serve without bond or other surety. If the aforementioned person does not qualify, or ceases to serve, I name _____ as my alternate Executor, also to serve without bond or other surety.

I grant that my Executor take all actions legally permissible to probate this Will. These powers shall include all actions as my Executor deems to be in the best interests of my estate which shall include, but not be limited to, the following:

(A) To employ accountants, attorneys, investment counsel, agents, banks, or trust companies (collectively, "Professionals") to perform services for and at the expense of my estate. My Executor is expressly relieved of any liability or responsibility whatsoever for any act or failure to act by, or for following the advice of, any Professionals so long as my Executor exercises due care in their selection. Any compensation paid pursuant to this subparagraph shall not affect in any manner the amount of or the right of my Executor to receive compensation as my fiduciary.

(B) To retain any real or personal property, without liability for loss or depreciation resulting from such retention.

(C) To sell, exchange, or lease for any period of time, any real or personal property.

(D) To purchase all forms of property, including but not limited to stocks, bonds, notes and other securities, real estate, or any variety of real or personal property, without being confined to so-called legal investments and without regard for the principle of diversification.

(E) To deal with and settle claims in favor of or against my estate without order of court.

(F) To vote stock; to convert bonds, notes, stocks, or other securities belonging to my estate into other securities; and to exercise all other rights and privileges of a person owning similar property.

(G) To continue, maintain, operate, or participate in any business which is a part of my estate, and to incorporate, dissolve, or otherwise change the form of organization of the business.

(H) To pay all debts and taxes that may be assessed against my estate, as provided under state law.

Your initials*: _____
Witness #1 initials: _____
Witness #2 initials: _____
Witness #3 initials: _____
*sign your full name in Louisiana   Page _____ of _____

(I) To do all other acts which in my Executor's judgment may be necessary for the proper and advantageous management, investment, and distribution of my estate

Other instructions: _____

_____

7. Appointment of Guardians. I appoint the following, if needed.

Personal Guardian. If at the time of my death any of my children are minors and a personal guardian is needed, I appoint _____ as the personal guardian of my minor children, to serve without bond or other surety. If this person is unwilling or unable to serve as the personal guardian of my minor children, then I appoint _____ _____ as the personal guardian of my minor children, to serve without bond or other surety.

Property Guardian. If at the time of my death any of my children are minors and a property guardian is needed, I appoint _____ as the property guardian of my minor children, to serve without bond or other surety. If this person is unwilling or unable to serve as the property guardian of my minor children, then I appoint _____ as the property guardian of my minor children, to serve without bond or other surety.

Your initials*: _____
Witness #1 initials: _____
Witness #2 initials: _____
Witness #3 initials: _____
*sign your full name in Louisiana   Page _____ of _____

Will Section 8: Young Person's Trust. This section allows you to create a young person's trust. A "trust" is like an artificial person who holds money or property after you die in accordance with your instructions, for the benefit of other persons, called beneficiaries. Each trust has a trustee whose job it is to administer the money and property in the trust in accordance with rules you set up in the document that establishes the trust. You literally "trust" that the money or property will be handled as you specify.

Trusts can become extremely complex. However, our purpose is to give you the ability to create a simple and effective young person's trust to safeguard money or property you give to minors or young adults until they reach a level of maturity sufficient to manage the money or property themselves. Otherwise, you will lose all control when the minor or young adult to whom you left the money or property reaches the age of majority (eighteen or twenty-one, depending on the state).

If that's not a problem for you, you don't need a young person's trust. If, however, you would prefer that a trustee handle the money or property (or parts of it) until your beneficiary is older, then a young person's trust will be a valuable part of your estate plan.

Keep in mind that you can use a young person's trust even if your beneficiary is already an adult in the eyes of the law when the trust is set up. If, for instance, you want to give money to a twenty-two-year-old son or nephew, but you don't want him to have full use of the money until he is thirty, you can use the young person's trust form that follows for this purpose.

If you don't want to create a young person's trust write "not applicable" in the blanks on the form, making it clear that you failed to fill in these provisions on purpose. Use your extra copy of this form in the event that you wish to create a young person's trust at some future time.

Here is what you need to know in order to complete the form for a young person's trust, should you choose to establish one.

Introduction. This provision explains that you are establishing a separate trust for each beneficiary named in this section of your will. There is nothing to add or delete here.

Trust Beneficiaries and Age When Young Person's Trust Shall End. Here is where you should write the names of each beneficiary for whom you are establishing the trust, and the age at which the money and/or property being held in the trust should be released to the beneficiary.

Appointment of Trustee. The trustee's main responsibilities are to act honestly and manage each young person's property. This entails making prudent investments of trust assets, keeping good financial records, timely filing of annual state and federal trust income tax returns, and distributing the trust income and principal as deemed necessary for the young person's benefit. This form also gives the trustee the right to use the assets in the young person's trust for each beneficiary's "health, education, maintenance, and support."

You may name any person over age nineteen who is U.S. citizen as the trustee. You may also name a U.S. corporation possessed of trust powers (like banks and trust companies, though this may be more expensive). As mentioned previously, in order to consolidate all financial responsibilities, it may make good sense to use the same person named as the property guardian. The surviving parent, if there is one, does not have the automatic right to serve as trustee of the young person's trust, so if this is your desire, say so, and make certain to name an alternate trustee in the event that, for instance, you and the other parent die simultaneously.

Trust Provisions. This provision specifies exactly how your trustee is to distribute income and principal for the benefit of each young person who is a trust beneficiary. It also provides that the trust terminates when the beneficiary reaches the age you designate in the trust, or if the beneficiary dies before reaching that age. Upon termination, the remaining trust principal and accumulated net income will pass to your choice of the beneficiary's heirs, in equal shares, or to your surviving children, in equal shares. There are blank lines provided for this decision, and you must initial your choice.

Trustee Powers. This provision specifies standard powers of your trustee. There is nothing to add or delete here.

Trust Administration Provisions. This provision specifies standard administration provisions to assure the smooth functioning of your trust. Importantly, it contains a "spendthrift clause"—language that will help to protect the trust property from the beneficiary's creditors. There is nothing to add or delete here.

Now turn the page and complete section 8 of your will.

8. Young Person's Trust

The term "beneficiary" in the following trust provisions shall mean the young person (as "young person" is specified in Subsection A of this Young Person's Trust) for whom the Young Person's Trust is being administered. My Trustee shall hold, administer, and distribute all property passing under this Will to a beneficiary, or passing to my Trustee for the benefit of a beneficiary, in separate trusts (the "Young Person's Trust"), one trust per beneficiary, as follows:

A. Trust Beneficiaries and Age When Young Person's Trust Shall End

Each Young Person's Trust shall end when the following beneficiaries become thirty-five years of age, unless sooner specified below.

Beneficiary   Age Trust Shall End

_____   _____

_____   _____

_____   _____

_____   _____

B. Appointment of Trustee

I name _____ as Trustee, to serve without bond or other surety. If this person is unwilling or unable to serve as Trustee, I name _____ to serve as alternate Trustee, also to serve without bond or other surety.

C. Trust Provisions

(1) Until the termination date, my Trustee shall distribute to or for the benefit of each beneficiary as much of the net income and principal as my Trustee deems necessary for the beneficiary's health, education, maintenance, and support, annually adding to principal undistributed income.

(2) The Young Person's Trust shall terminate upon the occurrence of any of the following:

    (a) The beneficiary attains the age specified in Subsection A above of this Trust.

    (b) The beneficiary dies before the age specified in Subsection A above of this Trust.

    (c) The trust property is entirely consumed.

(3) Upon termination of this Young Person's Trust, the remaining trust principal and accumulated income shall pass to the beneficiary, if alive. In the event the beneficiary is not alive, I direct the remaining trust principal and accumulated income pass as follows:

(I have placed my initials next to the one provision below that I adopt as part of this Will. The unmarked provision is not adopted by me and is not part of this Will):

    _____ To the lineal descendants of the predeceased beneficiary, per stirpes

    _____ Equally to the other surviving named beneficiaries specified in Subsection

A above of this Trust, to be combined with and administered as part of any then existing Young Person's Trust created under this Will for the benefit of such named beneficiaries.

Your initials*:   _____
Witness #1 initials: _____
Witness #2 initials: _____
Witness #3 initials: _____
*sign your full name in Louisiana   Page _____ of _____

D. Trustee Powers

In addition to the other powers granted to the Trustee in this Will, the Trustee shall have all powers generally conferred on Trustees under the laws of the state having jurisdiction over this Young Person's Trust. The Trustee shall also have all powers conferred on my Executor in Section 6 of this Will. Additionally, the Trustee shall have all powers to hire and pay from the assets of the Young Person's Trust reasonable fees necessary to administer the Young Person's Trust and manage any asset of the Young Person's Trust.

E. Trust Provisions

(1) The situs of each of the Young Person's Trusts created hereunder may be selected by the Trustee in his or her sole discretion, and may be changed from time to time by the Trustee.

(2) The interests of the Young Person's Trust beneficiaries shall not be transferable by voluntary or involuntary assignment or by operation of law and shall be free from the claims of creditors and from attachment, execution, bankruptcy, or other legal process to the fullest extent permissible by law.

3) Any Trustee serving shall be entitled to reasonable compensation for his or her services. Any corporate Trustee (if appointed) shall be entitled to receive compensation for its services in an amount to be determined from time to time by the application of the current prevailing rates then charged by such corporate Trustee for estates or trusts of a similar size and character, and if such corporate Trustee shall be required to render extraordinary services, it shall be entitled to receive additional compensation for such

(4) The alternate Trustee then serving may appoint in writing an individual or a corporation possessed of trust powers to succeed him or her as Trustee, and such appointment shall become effective when accepted by such successor Trustee.

(5) Upon sixty (60) days prior notice to the Trust beneficiary, any Trustee serving hereunder may resign without the approval of a court or any Trust beneficiary provided that after such resignation there shall remain at least one Trustee.

(6) If no Trustee(s) is serving, then a replacement Trustee to fill such vacancy shall be appointed by the adult beneficiary of the Trust, or, by the Guardian of such beneficiary if a minor.

(7) Any successor Trustee, however appointed, shall be relieved of any and all liability for any acts or omissions of the predecessor Trustees in respect to the administration of this Trust and may, without liability, accept without examination or review the accounts rendered and the property delivered by any predecessor Trustee.

Your initials*: _____
Witness #1 initials: _____
Witness #2 initials: _____
Witness #3 initials: _____
*sign your full name in Louisiana   Page _____ of _____

Will Section 9: Survival Clause. See the coordinate section in the short-form will, explained in Chapter Four.

Will Section 10: Construction. See the coordinate section in the short-form will, explained in Chapter Four.

Will Section 11: Definitions. See the coordinate section in the short-form will, explained in Chapter Four.

Will Section 12: Severability. See the coordinate section in the short-form will, explained in Chapter Four.

Will Section 13: Optional Provisions. See the coordinate section in the short-form will, explained in Chapter Four.

Will Section 14: Signature Line. See the coordinate section in the short-form will, explained in Chapter Four. REMEMBER NOT TO SIGN YOUR WILL YET.

Now turn the page and initial the optional provisions as you desire.

9. Survival Clause

If any beneficiary of this Will, including my spouse, if any, and including any beneficiary of any trust established by this Will, shall die within sixty days of my death, I hereby declare that I shall be deemed to have survived such person.

10. Construction

As used herein, the terms "Testator" and "Executor" are meant to refer to either gender or both, singular and plural.

11. Definitions

"Spouse" shall mean the person named as my Spouse in Section 2, or if not so named, the person to whom I am legally married at the time of my death; provided, however, if my Spouse is divorced from me or living separate from me at time of my death, my Spouse shall be treated as if he or she predeceased me.

12. Severability

If any part of this Will is declared invalid, illegal, or inoperative for any reason, it is my intent that the remaining parts shall be effective and fully operative, and that any Court so interpreting this Will and any provision in it construe in favor of survival.

13. Optional Provisions

I have placed my initials next to the provisions below that I adopt as part of this Will. Any unmarked provision is not adopted by me and is not a part of this Will.

_____ I desire to be buried in the _____ cemetery located at _____.

_____ I direct that my remains be cremated and that the ashes be disposed of according to the wishes of my Executor.

_____ I direct that my remains be cremated and that the ashes be disposed of in the following manner: _____

_____.

14. Signature Line

I subscribe my name to this Will this ____ day of _____, _____, at _____, State of _____, and declare it is my last Will, that I sign it willingly, that I execute it as my free and voluntary act for the purposes expressed, and that I am of the age of majority or otherwise legally empowered to make a Will and under no constraint or undue influence.

Your initials*: _____
Witness #1 initials: _____
Witness #2 initials: _____
Witness #3 initials: _____
*sign your full name in Louisiana   Page _____ of _____

CHAPTER SIX

Finalizing and Signing Your Will

In order to assure the validity of your will, you must finalize it and sign it in accordance with the technical requirements explained in this chapter. Your will might still be valid if you fail to fully comply with these requirements, but then again it might not. For your peace of mind, you should follow these procedures carefully.

Read this chapter in its entirety before you begin the process of finalizing and signing your will.

STEP ONE: REVIEW YOUR WILL

Before you prepare to sign your will make sure that what you wrote in the blanks clearly and accurately reflects your intent. If you can, have a trusted friend read it—what may be clear to you may not be clear to someone else.

As we have stated previously, make sure there are no cross-outs, alterations, or obvious erasures in your will. If there is a provision that you purposefully left blank, write "not applicable" on each line in order to make plain that it was not left blank by mistake.

STEP TWO: HAVE THREE WITNESSES IN ATTENDANCE

You will need three witnesses who actually see you sign your will. The witnesses must then sign a witness statement form, which will be attached to your will. The witness statement form is included after step three, below. The purpose of the witness

statement form is to provide a place for your witnesses to verify that they saw you sign your will, and for the witnesses to provide their addresses so they can be located in the future if required.

In addition, you should sign a self-proving affidavit form in the presence of your witnesses, who will then also sign the form. Like the witness statement, the self-proving affidavit form will also be attached to your will. It, too, is included after step three, below. The self-proving affidavit takes its name from the fact that if properly signed and attached to your will, it may (depending on the state in which you live when you die) eliminate the requirement that your witnesses appear in court after your death to swear that they saw you sign your will. Otherwise, your survivors will have to track down the persons who witnessed your will and get them into the courthouse, perhaps decades after the fact, assuming they are still alive. In any case, the self-proving affidavit form provides an extra layer of authentication that is always a good idea.

In every state except Vermont only two witnesses are required, but it is always best to have an extra witness, just in case you cannot locate a witness, or the signature of one of your witnesses is challenged or invalidated for some reason.

ALERT: **Your witnesses should be at least twenty-one years of age, and must have no interest in the will. Different states define when a witness is "interested" in different ways, but be** very careful if a witness stands to inherit anything under the will, or if the witness is named as executor, trustee, or guardian, or if the witness would inherit property from the decedent under state law if the will were invalidated, or if the witness is the spouse of someone who has an interest under the will.

STEP THREE: SIGNING THE WILL, THE WITNESS STATEMENT, AND THE SELF-PROVING AFFIDAVIT

To properly sign all of the required documents, you and your witnesses will need to meet with a notary public. You can usually find a notary public in the telephone book. If you have a relationship with a bank (or, for instance, you plan on storing your will in a safe deposit box at a bank), the bank will often make the services of a notary public available.

In the presence of all of the witnesses and the notary public, sign and date your will where indicated. Then write your initials at the bottom of every page of the will, where indicated. Make sure your witnesses see you write your signature and your initials. Your witnesses do not need to read your will and they do not need to know anything about its contents. However, they do need to know that the document you are signing is your will, and they need to actually see you sign it and initial it. (Note that if you live in Louisiana, instead of initialing the bottom of every page, you must sign your full name at the bottom of every page, and you must do so in the presence of the witnesses and the notary public.)

You will then need to complete the witness statement form. A version of the witness statement form that will work in all states appears on the next page. (Note that the "Testator" referred to in this form is you, the person making the will.) Have each of your witnesses sign the witness statement where indicated. Make sure that you, the notary public, and each witness watches as this is being done. Also make sure that each of your witnesses fills in the blanks on the witness statement—printing their names, addresses, and so on.

Finally, you should initial (or in Louisiana, sign) where indicated at the bottom of the page, and each of the witnesses should also write their initials where indicated at the bottom of the page.

Witness Statement

On this _____ day of _____, _____, the Testator _____, declared to us, the undersigned, that this instrument was his or her Will and requested us to act as witnesses to it. The Testator signed this Will in our presence, all of us being present at the same time. We now, at the Testator's request, in the Testator's presence and in the presence of each other, subscribe our names as witnesses and each declare that we are of sound mind and of proper age to witness a Will. We further declare that we understand this to be the Testator's Will, and that to the best of out knowledge the Testator is of the age of majority, or is otherwise legally empowered to make a Will, and appears to be of sound mind and under no constraint or undue influence.

We declare under penalty of perjury that the foregoing is true and correct, this

_____ day of _____, _____, at _____, State of _____.

_____   _____
(witness' signature)   (printed name)

residing at _____, _____
(street address)   (city)

_____, _____
(county)   (state)

_____   _____
(witness' signature)   (printed name)

residing at _____, _____
(street address)   (city)

_____, _____
(county)   (state)

_____   _____
(witness' signature)   (printed name)

residing at _____, _____
(street address)   (city)

_____, _____
(county)   (state)

Your initials*:   _____
Witness #1 initials: _____
Witness #2 initials: _____
Witness #3 initials: _____
*sign your full name in Louisiana   Page _____ of _____

Various states use different self-proving affidavit forms. The following pages will instruct you as to which form works in your state. A few states (California, the District of Columbia, Maryland, Michigan, Ohio, and Vermont, at latest count) either do not have a law authorizing self-proving affidavits or do not make forms available, but even if you live in one of these states it is still a good idea to sign one of these forms—the first form below is the most widely accepted, so use that.

Have each of your witnesses sign the self-proving affidavit where indicated. Make sure that the notary public watches as this is being done. The notary public will have you and the witnesses swear to the truth of the statements in the self-proving affidavit. The notary public will then sign and affix a notary seal to the self-proving affidavit.

When this has been completed, you should initial (or in Louisiana, sign) where indicated at the bottom of each page, and the witnesses should each write their initials where indicated at the bottom of each page.

Note that in these forms, you, the person making the will, are referred to as the "testator" (if male) or the "testatrix" (if female).

Use the following form if you live in any of these states:

Alabama	Maine	Ohio
Alaska	Maryland	Oregon
Arkansas	Michigan	South Carolina
California	Minnesota	South Dakota
Colorado	Mississippi	Tennessee
Connecticut	Montana	Utah
District of Columbia	Nebraska	Vermont
Hawaii	Nevada	Washington
Idaho	New Mexico	West Virginia
Illinois	New York	
Indiana	North Dakota	

Self-Proving Affidavit

STATE OF _____

COUNTY OF _____

We, _____, and _____, _____, and _____, the testator or testatrix and the witnesses, whose names are signed to the attached or foregoing instrument in those capacities, personally appearing before the under-signed authority and being first duly sworn, declare to the undersigned authority under penalty of perjury that 1) the testator or testatrix declared, signed, and executed the instrument as his or her last Will; 2) he or she signed it willingly, or directed another to sign for him or her; 3) he or she executed it as his or her free and voluntary act for the purposes therein expressed; and 4) each of the witnesses, the request of the testator or testatrix, in his or her hearing and presence and in the presence of each other, signed the Will as witnesses, and that to the best of his or her knowledge the testator or testatrix was at that time of full legal age, of sound mind, and under no constraint or undue influence.

_____(Testator or Testatrix)

_____(Witness)

_____(Witness)

_____(Witness)

Subscribed, sworn, and acknowledged before me, _____, a notary public, and by _____, the testator or testatrix, and by _____, and by _____, _____, and _____, witnesses, this _____ day of _____, _____.

_____
Notary Public

Your initials*: _____
Witness #1 initials: _____
Witness #2 initials: _____
Witness #3 initials: _____
*sign your full name in Louisiana   Page _____ of _____

Use the first form if you live in any of these states:

Delaware	Massachusetts	Pennsylvania
Florida	Missouri	Rhode Island
Georgia	New Jersey	Virginia
Iowa	North Carolina	Wyoming
Kansas	Oklahoma	Wisconsin
Kentucky		

Use the second form that follows this page if you live in New Hampshire.

Use the third form that follows this page if you live in Texas.

Self-Proving Affidavit

STATE OF _____

COUNTY OF _____

I, the undersigned, an officer authorized to administer oaths, certify that _____, the testator or testatrix, and _____, _____, and _____, the witnesses, whose names are signed to the attached or foregoing instrument and whose signatures appear below, having appeared before me and having been first been duly sworn, each then declared to me that 1) the attached or foregoing instrument is the last Will of the testator or testatrix; 2) the testator or testatrix willingly and voluntarily declared, signed, and executed the Will in the presence of the witnesses; 3) the witnesses signed the Will upon the request of the testator or testatrix, in the presence and hearing of the testator or testatrix and in the presence of each other; 4) to the best knowledge of each witness, the testator or testatrix was, at the time of signing, of the age of majority (or otherwise legally competent to make a Will), of sound mind and memory, and under no constraint or undue influence; and 5) each witness was and is competent and of proper age to witness a Will.

_____(Testator or Testatrix)

_____(Witness)

_____(Witness)

_____(Witness)

Subscribed and sworn to before me by that _____, the testator or testatrix, who is personally known to me or who has produced a _____ as identification, and by _____, a witness, who is personally known to me or who has produced a _____ as identification, and by _____, a witness, who is personally known to me or who has produced a _____ ___as identification, and by _____ a witness, who is personally known to me or who has produced a _____ as identification, this ____ day of _____, _____.

_____
Notary Public

Your initials*: _____
Witness #1 initials: _____
Witness #2 initials: _____
Witness #3 initials: _____
*sign your full name in Louisiana   Page _____ of _____

Self-Proving Affidavit

STATE OF NEW HAMPSHIRE

COUNTY OF _____

The foregoing instrument was acknowledged before me this _____[day], by
_____, the testator or testatrix; _____,
_____, and _____, the witnesses, who under oath swear as
follows:

1. The testator or testatrix signed the instrument as his or her Will or expressly directed another to sign for him or her.

2. This was the testator or testatrix's free and voluntary act for the purposes expressed in the Will.

3. Each witness signed at the request of the testator or testatrix, in his or her presence, and in the presence of the other witness.

4. To the best of my knowledge, at the time of the signing the testator or testatrix was at least eighteen years of age, or if under eighteen years was a married person, and was of sane mind and under no constraint or undue influence.

_____
Signature

_____
Official Capacity

Your initials*:   _____
Witness #1 initials: _____
Witness #2 initials: _____
Witness #3 initials: _____
*sign your full name in Louisiana   Page _____ of _____

Self-Proving Affidavit

STATE OF TEXAS

COUNTY OF

Before me, the undersigned authority, on this day personally appeared _____ _____, _____, and _____, known to me to be the testator or testatrix and the witnesses, respectively, whose names are subscribed to the annexed or foregoing instrument in their respective capacities, and, all of said persons being by me duly sworn, the said _____ testator or testatrix, declared to me and to the said witnesses in my presence that said instrument is his or her last Will and testament, and that he or she had willingly made and executed it as his or her free act and deed, and the said witnesses, each on his or her oath stated to me in the presence and hearing of the said testator or testatrix, that the said testator or testatrix had declared to them that said instrument is his or her last Will and testament, and that each witness stated further that they did sign the same as witnesses in the presence of the said testator or testatrix and at his or her request; that he or she was at the time eighteen years of age or over (or being under such age, was or had been lawfully married, or was then a member of the armed forces of the United States or an auxiliary thereof or of the Maritime service) and was of sound mind; and that each of said witnesses was then at least fourteen years of age.

_____ (Testator or Testatrix)

(Witness)_____

(Witness)_____

(Witness)_____

Subscribed and sworn to before me by _____, the testator or testatrix, and by _____, _____ and _____ the witnesses, this _____ day of _____, 20___.

Signed: _____

Your initials*: _____
Witness #1 initials: _____
Witness #2 initials: _____
Witness #3 initials: _____
*sign your full name in Louisiana   Page _____ of _____

STEP FOUR: NUMBER THE PAGES WHERE INDICATED

Count the number of pages in your will, including the signed witness statement and self-proving affidavit forms. Then number every one of these pages, using the preprinted format "___ of ___" at the bottom of each page, where the first blank is the page number and the second is the total number of pages, as in "4 of 9." This is important: numbering the pages in this way will remove any doubt that your survivors may have about whether this comprises your entire Will.

STEP FIVE: STORING YOUR WILL

You should not have more than one original of your will. Doing so can complicate matters if you wish to create a new will at a later time, as it may prove difficult to track down all copies of your old will. It may also cause problems if you keep photocopies of your signed will. Instead, if you are comfortable doing so, consider providing your beneficiaries, or your executor and alternate executor, with an unsigned copy of your will.

As discussed previously, leave all of the will pages in this book. Keep this book in a safe place, and let your family members, friends, and/or executor and alternate executor know where you have stored it. A safe deposit box is ideal.

If you have previously executed a different will, physically destroy it along with all copies of it.

STEP SIX: PERIODICALLY REVIEW YOUR WILL AND YOUR ASSET WORKSHEETS

Keep your will current. The form wills in this book anticipate certain predictable events, but they cannot account for all changes in your preferences, your needs, your assets, or your family situation. For instance:

◆ If you used the short-form will, think about whether you now need to use the long-form will.

◆ If you have accumulated additional assets, think about whether you wish to add bequests, or if you wish to divide your residue among additional beneficiaries. If you gave bequests of property to specific persons, but have since sold that property, you may want to provide for those persons in another way.

◆ If you are married, you may want to verify that you have left a sufficient percentage of your probate and nonprobate assets to your spouse, particularly if you think your spouse might challenge your will after you die. If you are now separated or divorced, you will want to review your will carefully.

◆ Think about whether you remain satisfied with your choice of executor, guardian, and trustee. Think about whether you are satisfied with the beneficiary designations on any life insurance policies, annuity contracts, bank accounts, IRAs, 401(k)s, and other retirement accounts.

◆ If you established a young person's trust for your first child, and then have a second child, you may want to include your second child in the trust.

◆ If the value of your nonprobate assets has declined, you may want to make provisions in your will for persons who will not be receiving as much nonprobate property as you had originally planned. On the other hand, if it has increased, you may want to make other adjustments.

◆ If you think your assets have increased to the point where you might incur estate taxes, or if you have started a business, or if a child has developed some health concerns, you may need some professional planning.

Remember not to make changes on the face of a will you already completed. Use the extra blank forms you made before you began, as instructed in Chapter One.

CHAPTER SEVEN

Your Health-Care Power of Attorney

Most people have heard of a "living will," but not everyone knows exactly what it is—and is not.

The term "living will" is a misnomer—it is not a will, and it is not part of your will. It is a separate document that lets your family members and medical providers know what type of care you do and do not want to receive if you are unable to speak for yourself at the terminal stage of your life. Generally speaking, a living will allows you to make the decision now to specifically decline various procedures and measures, such as the artificial administration of food and fluids and cardiopulmonary resuscitation.

This book does not include a living will, for the reason that there is no single living will form that is acceptable in each state. To find a form that works in your state, check your state's website—some, but not all, states will provide a form you can download. In addition, the National Hospice and Palliative Care Organization sponsors a website, www.caringinfo.org, that provides many state forms and other useful information.

Instead of a living will, however, this book includes a health-care power of attorney form, which is in many respects much more useful and effective than a living will.

A health-care power of attorney gives another person the authority to carry out your wishes when you are unable to speak for yourself, even if you are not yet in the final stages of life. As such, it becomes effective before a living will, which only applies when your condition becomes terminal. As soon as a physician concludes that you are unable to make your own decisions, the person you designate in your health-care power of attorney, typically referred to as your "agent," can act on your behalf in a variety of situations. If you regain the ability to make decisions, your agent's authority ceases.

There's another advantage as well. Like a living will, the form used in this book empowers you to deal with end-of-life decisions—you can instruct your agent as to your wishes. But unlike a living will, your agent will also be empowered to interpret your wishes when the situation is not so black and white, and to deal with the kinds of circumstances you could not have foreseen.

There is, however, one advantage a living will has over a health-care power of attorney. A living will does not require you to appoint an agent—the living will document does the talking regarding your end-of-life preferences. Therefore, if you do not have someone you trust to be your agent, you should consider utilizing a living will.

Thankfully, most states no longer insist that you use only their "official" living will forms. If you see a provision in another state's form that you like, you will most likely be able to include it in your form. Just make sure that your living will is signed and witnessed in compliance with your state's requirements. Reviewing these alternatives may also provide you with some ideas for your health-care power of attorney. There is no "one size fits all" approach to these decisions, and the more thought you devote to these difficult issues, the better.

INSTRUCTIONS FOR COMPLETING YOUR HEALTH CARE POWER OF ATTORNEY

Here's how to complete your health-care power of attorney.

Choose an Agent and an Alternate Agent. Your first decision involves the choice of your agent, and an alternate agent should your primary agent become unwilling or unable to serve. When deciding who to designate as your agent, you should consider the following:

The person designated as your agent cannot be one of the following:

◆ a minor (but note that some states define a minor as a person under the age of twenty-one, so your agent must also be at least twenty-one years of age);
◆ your attending physician;
◆ an employee of your attending physician; or
◆ an employee of a health-care facility in which you are a patient if the employee is providing direct patient care to you or is an officer, director, partner, or business office employee of a health-care facility or of any parent organization of the health-care facility.

Otherwise, choosing an agent and alternate agent is a highly personal decision. Most married persons choose their spouse. Note that if you designate your spouse and later become divorced or legally separated (a "legal separation" is a status recognized in some, but not all, states), this form will terminate your spouse's authority to act as your agent and give all authority to your alternate agent. Younger, unmarried persons often choose a parent. In other instances, you obviously want to choose someone whose judgment you can trust in the most difficult of circumstances, and who will respect your preferences even if those preferences may violate their own beliefs.

Discuss your Preferences. One of the benefits of a health-care power of attorney is that it allows your agent to make judgment calls when confronted with difficult situations. Your agent will likely be discussing these crucial issues with your family and physician if and when the time comes. To increase the likelihood that your agent will make the same decision you would have made, discuss your values, the medical issues likely to arise, and your preferences with your agent, your alternate agent and your close family members. Involve your physician in these discussions so that all concerned can learn more about the issues and options.

Fill in the Blanks. There are various blanks in the health-care power of attorney form that you must fill in. They will be self-explanatory—each blank will be preceded or followed by instructions.

Note that on page 2 of the form, you must enter the legal citation for the applicable law in the state in which you reside. As instructed in the form, this requires you to consult the appendix to the health-care power of attorney. Whatever is listed for your state should be entered on this line exactly as it appears in the appendix.

ALERT: **The form used in this book does not comply with Oregon law. Residents of Oregon should obtain the correct Oregon form from a state official or attorney. Additionally note that the form also includes a page for Wisconsin residents only. If you reside in any other state, this page should be eliminated from the form. In all other respects, this form has been designed to be valid in all other states.**

In addition, while this form provides your agent with general powers to act on your behalf for purposes of your health care, it also allows you to specifically list your values, wishes, and desires if you so choose. If you desire to limit your agent's powers or to provide him or her with written guidance, be sure to add language to reflect your wishes more accurately where indicated on the form.

Sign the Health-Care Power of Attorney. When you are ready to sign the document, you must do it in front of two witnesses and a notary public. Most, but not all, states require two completely disinterested witnesses and a disinterested notary. States differ on who is "disinterested" and otherwise qualified to serve as a witness or notary public for this purpose. In order to comply with the most stringent state requirements, it is important that none of the following serve as witnesses or as notary public:

◆ a minor (again noting that the person should be at least twenty-one years of age);
◆ the person you have designated as your agent or alternate agent;
◆ a person related to you by blood or marriage;
◆ a person entitled to any part of your estate after your death under a will or codicil executed by you, a person entitled to any part of your estate by operation of law;
◆ your attending physician;
◆ an employee of your attending physician;
◆ an employee of a health-care facility in which you are a patient if the employee is providing direct patient care to you or is an officer, director, partner, or business office employee of a health-care facility or of any parent organization of the health-care facility;
◆ a person who, at the time this power of attorney is executed, has a claim against any part of your estate after your death.

Have Your Agent and Alternate Agent Sign the Acceptance Form. Also included in this form is an acceptance by health-care agent form that must be signed by your agent and alternate agent.

To Whom Should You Give Copies? Leave the original of your completed health-care power of attorney in this book. The "To Whom It May Concern" page at the beginning of the book instructs your agent and family members where to find it and what to do with it. You should, however, provide copies to your agent and alternate agent, your close family members, your physicians, and any health-care facilities where you are being treated or may be treated. A copy should also be sent to your attorney, and a copy should be kept where you store your important papers.

Reviewing Your Health-Care Power of Attorney. Your health-care power of attorney can be revoked, replaced, or changed at any time, so long as your are still capable of making your own decisions. It is recommended that it be reviewed and revised as appropriate at least every two years, or as your health status changes. As noted in Chapter One, never make erasures, strike-outs, or alterations on your completed health-care power of attorney. Be certain that you always have at least one photocopy of the blank form stored in this book, and when you need to make revisions, do so on a blank form.

ALERT: **Some states, including Alabama, Arkansas, Georgia, Iowa, Pennsylvania, and others, will not recognize health-care power of attorney for women who are pregnant, even if the forms are completed in full compliance with the law.**

Your health-care power of attorney begins on the following page.

HEALTH-CARE POWER OF ATTORNEY

NOTICE TO PERSON MAKING THIS DOCUMENT

YOU HAVE THE RIGHT TO MAKE DECISIONS ABOUT YOUR HEATH CARE. NO HEALTH CARE MAY BE GIVEN TO YOU OVER YOUR OBJECTION, AND NECESSARY HEALTH CARE MAY NOT BE STOPPED OR WITHHELD IF YOU OBJECT.

BECAUSE YOUR HEALTH CARE PROVIDERS IN SOME CASES MAY NOT HAVE HAD THE OPPORTUNITY TO ESTABLISH A LONG-TERM RELATIONSHIP WITH YOU, THEY ARE OFTEN UNFAMILIAR WITH YOUR BELIEFS AND VALUES AND THE DETAILS OF YOUR FAMILY RELATIONSHIPS. THIS POSES A PROBLEM IF YOU BECOME PHYSICALLY OR MENTALLY UNABLE TO MAKE DECISIONS ABOUT YOUR HEALTH CARE.

IN ORDER TO AVOID THIS PROBLEM, YOU MAY SIGN THIS LEGAL DOCUMENT TO SPECIFY THE PERSON WHOM YOU WANT TO MAKE HEALTH-CARE DECISIONS FOR YOU IF YOU ARE UNABLE TO MAKE THOSE DECISIONS PERSONALLY. THAT PERSON IS KNOWN AS YOUR HEALTH-CARE AGENT. YOU SHOULD TAKE SOME TIME TO DISCUSS YOUR THOUGHTS AND BELIEFS ABOUT MEDICAL TREATMENT WITH THE PERSON OR PERSONS WHOM YOU HAVE SPECIFIED. YOU MAY STATE IN THIS DOCUMENT ANY TYPES OF HEALTH CARE THAT YOU DO OR DO NOT DESIRE, AND YOU MAY LIMIT THE AUTHORITY OF YOUR HEALTH-CARE AGENT. IF YOUR HEALTH-CARE AGENT IS UNAWARE OF YOUR DESIRES WITH RESPECT TO A PARTICULAR HEALTH-CARE DECISION, HE OR SHE IS REQUIRED TO DETERMINE WHAT WOULD BE IN YOUR BEST INTEREST IN MAKING THE DECISION.

THIS IS AN IMPORTANT LEGAL DOCUMENT. IT GIVES YOUR AGENT BROAD POWERS TO MAKE HEALTH CARE DECISIONS FOR YOU. IT REVOKES ANY PRIOR HEALTH-CARE POWER OF ATTORNEY THAT YOU MAY HAVE MADE. IF YOU WISH TO CHANGE YOUR HEALTH-CARE POWER OF ATTORNEY, YOU MAY REVOKE THIS DOCUMENT AT ANY TIME BY DESTROYING IT, BY DIRECTING ANOTHER PERSON TO DESTROY IT IN YOUR PRESENCE, BY SIGNING A WRITTEN AND DATED STATEMENT, OR BY STATING THAT IT IS REVOKED IN THE PRESENCE OF TWO WITNESSES. IF YOU REVOKE, YOU SHOULD NOTIFY YOUR AGENT, YOUR HEALTH-CARE PROVIDERS, AND ANY OTHER PERSON TO WHOM YOU HAVE GIVEN A COPY. IF YOUR AGENT IS YOUR SPOUSE AND YOUR MARRIAGE IS ANNULLED OR YOU ARE DIVORCED AFTER SIGNING THIS DOCUMENT, THE DOCUMENT IS INVALID.

YOU MAY ALSO USE THIS DOCUMENT TO MAKE OR REFUSE TO MAKE AN ANATOMICAL GIFT UPON YOUR DEATH. IF YOU USE THIS DOCUMENT TO MAKE OR REFUSE TO MAKE AN ANATOMICAL GIFT, THIS DOCUMENT REVOKES ANY PRIOR DOCUMENT OR GIFT THAT YOU MAY HAVE MADE. YOU MAY REVOKE OR CHANGE ANY ANATOMICAL GIFT THAT YOU MAKE BY THIS DOCUMENT BY CROSSING OUT THE ANATOMICAL GIFTS PROVISION IN THIS DOCUMENT.

DO NOT SIGN THIS DOCUMENT UNLESS YOU CLEARLY UNDERSTAND IT.

IT IS SUGGESTED THAT YOU KEEP THE ORIGINAL OF THIS DOCUMENT ON FILE WITH YOUR PHYSICIAN.

NOTICE TO PERSON MAKING THIS DOCUMENT

YOU HAVE THE RIGHT TO MAKE DECISIONS ABOUT YOUR HEALTH CARE. NO HEALTH CARE MAY BE GIVEN TO YOU OVER YOUR OBJECTION, AND NECESSARY HEALTH CARE MAY NOT BE STOPPED OR WITHHELD IF YOU OBJECT.

BECAUSE YOUR HEALTH-CARE PROVIDERS IN SOME CASES MAY NOT HAVE HAD THE OPPORTUNITY TO ESTABLISH A LONG-TERM RELATIONSHIP WITH YOU, THEY ARE OFTEN UNFAMILIAR WITH YOUR BELIEFS AND VALUES AND THE DETAILS OF YOUR FAMILY RELATIONSHIPS. THIS POSES A PROBLEM IF YOU BECOME PHYSICALLY OR MENTALLY UNABLE TO MAKE DECISIONS ABOUT YOUR HEALTH CARE.

IN ORDER TO AVOID THIS PROBLEM, YOU MAY SIGN THIS LEGAL DOCUMENT TO SPECIFY THE PERSON WHOM YOU WANT TO MAKE HEALTH-CARE DECISIONS FOR YOU IF YOU ARE UNABLE TO MAKE THOSE DECISIONS PERSONALLY. THAT PERSON IS KNOWN AS YOUR HEALTH-CARE AGENT. YOU SHOULD TAKE SOME TIME TO DISCUSS YOUR THOUGHTS AND BELIEFS ABOUT MEDICAL TREATMENT WITH THE PERSON OR PERSONS WHOM YOU HAVE SPECIFIED. YOU MAY STATE IN THIS DOCUMENT ANY TYPES OF HEALTH CARE THAT YOU DO OR DO NOT DESIRE, AND YOU MAY LIMIT THE AUTHORITY OF YOUR HEALTH-CARE AGENT. IF YOUR HEALTH-CARE AGENT IS UNAWARE OF YOUR DESIRES WITH RESPECT TO A PARTICULAR HEALTH-CARE DECISION, HE OR SHE IS REQUIRED TO DETERMINE WHAT WOULD BE IN YOUR BEST INTERESTS IN MAKING THE DECISION.

THIS IS AN IMPORTANT LEGAL DOCUMENT. IT GIVES YOUR AGENT BROAD POWERS TO MAKE HEALTH-CARE DECISIONS FOR YOU. IT REVOKES ANY PRIOR HEALTH-CARE POWER OF ATTORNEY THAT YOU MAY HAVE MADE. IF YOU WISH TO CHANGE YOUR HEALTH-CARE POWER OF ATTORNEY, YOU MAY REVOKE THIS DOCUMENT AT ANY TIME BY DESTROYING IT, BY DIRECTING ANOTHER PERSON TO DESTROY IT IN YOUR PRESENCE, BY SIGNING A WRITTEN AND DATED STATEMENT, OR BY STATING THAT IT IS REVOKED IN THE PRESENCE OF TWO WITNESSES. IF YOU REVOKE, YOU SHOULD NOTIFY YOUR AGENT, YOUR HEALTH-CARE PROVIDERS, AND ANY OTHER PERSON TO WHOM YOU HAVE GIVEN A COPY. IF YOUR AGENT IS YOUR SPOUSE AND YOUR MARRIAGE IS ANNULLED OR YOU ARE DIVORCED AFTER SIGNING THIS DOCUMENT, THE DOCUMENT IS INVALID.

YOU MAY ALSO USE THIS DOCUMENT TO MAKE OR REFUSE TO MAKE AN ANATOMICAL GIFT UPON YOUR DEATH. IF YOU USE THIS DOCUMENT TO MAKE OR REFUSE TO MAKE AN ANATOMICAL GIFT, THIS DOCUMENT REVOKES ANY PRIOR DOCUMENT OF GIFT THAT YOU MAY HAVE MADE. YOU MAY REVOKE OR CHANGE ANY ANATOMICAL GIFT THAT YOU MAKE BY THIS DOCUMENT BY CROSSING OUT THE ANATOMICAL GIFTS PROVISION IN THIS DOCUMENT.

DO NOT SIGN THIS DOCUMENT UNLESS YOU CLEARLY UNDERSTAND IT.

IT IS SUGGESTED THAT YOU KEEP THE ORIGINAL OF THIS DOCUMENT ON FILE WITH YOUR PHYSICIAN.

DESIGNATION OF HEALTH-CARE AGENT

I, _____ (insert your name)

(the "Principal") of_____

(insert your address)

being of sound mind, do hereby designate and appoint:

Name: _____

Address:_____

(Insert name, address, and telephone number of individual chosen as your health-care Agent.) as my Agent to make health-care decisions for me as authorized in this document. For the purpose of this document, "health-care decision" means consent, refusal of consent, or withdrawal of consent to any care, treatment, service, or procedure to maintain, diagnose, or treat an individual's physical condition.

CREATION OF HEALTH-CARE POWER OF ATTORNEY

By this document I intend to create a durable power of attorney for health care under _____). **(insert law applicable to your state as listed on the Appendix to this document)**. It is effective upon, and only during, any period of time in which I cannot make or communicate a choice regarding my health-care decisions, including end-of-life decisions. This power of attorney shall not be affected by my subsequent incapacity.

AUTHORITY GRANTED

Subject to any limitations in this document, I hereby grant to my Agent full power and authority to make health-care decisions for me to the same extent that I could make such decisions for myself if I had the capacity to do so. In exercising this authority, my Agent shall make health-care decisions that are consistent with my desires as stated in this document or otherwise made known to my Agent, including, but not limited to, my desires concerning obtaining or refusing or withdrawing life-prolonging care, treatment, services, and procedures. In making any decision, my Agent shall try to discuss the proposed decision with me to determine my desires, if possible and if those desires have not already been made known. If my Agent cannot determine my desires, my Agent shall make a choice based on what he/she believes to be in my best interest.

In the event that I am unable to provide informed consent for medical treatment and surgical and diagnostic procedures, and/or the withholding, withdrawal, or continuation of medical procedures, my Agent shall have the power to make all health-care decisions for me and to exercise all rights and powers concerning my care, custody, and treatment including, but not limited to, the following:

A. To consent, refuse, or withdraw consent to any and all types of health care;

B. To authorize my admission to or discharge (even against medical advice) from any hospital, nursing home, residential care, assisted living or similar facility or service;

C. To contract on my behalf for any health-care, related service or facility on my behalf, without my agent incurring personal financial liability for such contracts;

D. To hire and fire medical, social service, and other support personnel responsible for my care;

E. To authorize, or refuse to authorize, any medication or procedure intended to relieve pain, even though such use may lead to physical damage, addiction, or hasten the moment of (but not intentionally cause) my death;

F. To take any other action necessary to do what I authorize here, including (but not limited to) granting any waiver or release from liability required by any hospital, physician, or other health-care provider; signing any documents relating to refusals of treatment or the leaving of a facility against medical advice; and pursuing any legal action in my name at the expense of my estate to force compliance with my wishes as determined by my Agent, or to seek actual or punitive damages for the failure to comply.

STATEMENT OF DESIRES, SPECIAL PROVISIONS, AND LIMITATIONS

In exercising the authority under this document, my Agent shall act consistently with my desires concerning treatment, services, and procedures, including end-of-life decisions as stated below:

_____
_____
_____
_____
_____
_____
_____
_____
_____
_____
_____
_____
_____
_____
_____
_____

INSPECTION AND DISCLOSURE OF INFORMATION RELATING TO MY PHYSICAL OR MENTAL HEALTH

I further authorize my Agent to request, review, and receive any oral or written information regarding my physical or mental health, including medical and hospital records, and to execute any releases or other documents that may be required in order to obtain this information. I intend for any of my Agents, under this document, to be treated as I would be with respect to my rights regarding the use and disclosure of my individually identifiable health information or other medical records. This release authority applies to any information governed by the Health Insurance Portability and Accountability Act of 1996 ("HIPAA"), 42 U.S.C. 1320(d), 45 CFR 160-164. The authority given such agent above to request and receive such information will supersede any prior agreement I may have made with my health-care providers to restrict access to or disclosure of my individually identifiable health information. This authority given such Agent has no expiration date and will expire only in the event I revoke the authority in writing and deliver it to my health-care provider.

My Agent then serving shall be further authorized to execute on my behalf any releases or other documents that may be required in order to obtain my health-care records and consent to the disclosure of this information. I understand that any redisclosure of this information by my Agent may result in the information no longer being protected by federal law.

Any persons in possession of these records are authorized to release them to the designated Agent then serving upon presentation of this authorization or a photocopy thereof.

The purpose of the disclosure is to enable my Agent under this document to fully act as my personal representative under HIPAA, including the ability to access and rerelease my medical records. This authorization shall be deemed to comply with all requirements of HIPAA (45 CFR Section 164.509).

PROTECTION OF THIRD PARTIES WHO RELY ON MY AGENT

Any person who relies on good faith upon representations made by my Agent or Alternate Agent(s) then serving shall not be liable to me, my estate, my heirs, or assigns for their recognition of the Agent's authority to act on my behalf.

DESIGNATION OF ALTERNATE AGENTS

If :

A.   my then serving Agent dies, becomes incompetent, resigns, refuses to accept the office of Agent, becomes unwilling or unable to act;

B.   I revoke that person's appointment or authority to act as my Agent to make health-care decisions for me; or

C.   I become legally separated from or divorced from the Agent, if my spouse,

I designate and appoint the following persons to serve as alternates to my Agent, each of whom shall act alone and successively, in the order named:

A.   First Alternate Agent

Name:_____

Address:_____

Second Alternate Agent

Name:_____

Address:_____

PRIOR DESIGNATIONS REVOKED
I revoke any prior health-care power of attorney.

GUARDIANSHIP
In the event a guardian of my person is ever to be appointed by a Court, I nominate my Agent to serve as guardian of my person.

SEVERABILITY
If any provision of this document is ruled unenforceable, the remaining provisions shall stay in effect.

SIGNATURE OF PRINCIPAL

I, _____(insert name here), the Principal, sign my name to this Power of Attorney this _____ day of _____(insert month), _____ (insert year), and, being first duly sworn, do declare to the undersigned authority that I sign and execute this instrument as my power of attorney and that I sign it willingly, or willingly direct another to sign for me, that I execute it as my free and voluntary act for the purposes expressed in the power of attorney and that I am twenty-one years of age or older, of sound mind, and under no constraint or undue influence.

_____

(sign here)

STATEMENT OF WITNESSES

I declare under penalty of perjury under the laws of _____ (insert state of signing) that the person who signed this document, the Principal, is known to me, or proved to me on basis of satisfactory evidence to be the person whose name is subscribed to this instrument; that the Principal signed this Power of Attorney voluntarily and in my presence; that the Principal appears to be of sound mind and under no duress, fraud, or undue influence; that I am at least twenty-one (21) years of age; that I am not the person appointed as the Principal's Agent by this document; that I am not directly financially responsible for the Principal's health care; that I am not a health-care provider, an employee of a health-care provider, the operator of a health-care institution nor an employee of an operator of a health-care institution, the operator of a community care facility nor an employee of an operator of a community care facility; that I am not related to the Principal by blood, marriage, or adoption; and that, to the best of my knowledge, I do not, at the present time, have a claim to any portion of the estate of the principal upon the death of the Principal under a will or codicil thereto now existing, or by operation of law.

_____   _____
Signature   Signature

_____   _____
Print Name   Print Name

_____   _____
Residence address   Residence address

NOTARY

State of _____

County of_____

On this _____ day of _____, _____, before me personally

appeared_____(insert name of person giving power of attorney) known to me, or proved to me on basis of satisfactory evidence to be the person whose name is subscribed to this instrument, acknowledged that he/she executed it. I declare under penalty of perjury that the person whose name is subscribed to this instrument appears to be of sound mind and under no duress, fraud, or undue influence. I further declare that I am at least twenty-one (21) years of age; that I am not the person appointed as the Principal's Agent by this document; that I am not directly financially responsible for the Principal's health care; that I am not a health-care provider, an employee of a health-care provider, the operator of a health-care institution nor an employee of an operator of a health-care institution, the operator of a community care facility, nor an employee of an operator of a community care facility; that I am not related to the Principal by blood, marriage, or adoption; and that, to the best of my knowledge, I do not, at the present time, have a claim to any portion of the estate of the principal upon the death of the Principal under a will or codicil thereto now existing, or by operation of law.

_____
Signature of Notary

ACCEPTANCE BY HEALTH-CARE AGENT

A.   This designation shall not become effective unless the patient is unable to participate in treatment decisions.

B.   I shall not exercise powers concerning the Principal's care, custody, and medical treatment that the Principal, if able to participate in the decision, could not have exercised in his or her own behalf.

C.   This designation cannot be used to make a medical treatment decision to withhold or withdraw treatment from a Principal who is pregnant that would result in the pregnant Principal's death.

D.   I shall not receive compensation for the performance of my authority, rights, and responsibilities, but I may be reimbursed for actual and necessary expenses incurred in the performance of my authority, rights, and responsibilities.

E.   I shall act in accordance with the standards of care applicable to fiduciaries when acting for the Principal and shall act consistent with his or her best interests. The known desires of the Principal expressed or evidenced while the Principal is able to participate in medical treatment decisions are presumed to be in his or her best interests.

F.   The Principal may revoke his or her designation at any time or in any manner sufficient to communicate an intent to revoke.

G.   I may revoke my acceptance to the designation at any time and in any manner sufficient to communicate an intent to revoke.

I have read this document carefully, and have personally discussed with the Principal his or her health-care wishes at a time of possible incapacity. I further state that I am at least twenty-one (21) years of age and that I am not a health-care provider, an employee of a health-care provider, the operator of a health-care institution nor an employee of an operator of a health-care institution, the operator of a community care facility, nor an employee of an operator of a community care facility. If called upon and to the best of my ability, I will try to carry out the Principal's wishes as stated or made known to me.

I understand the above conditions and I accept the designation as health-care Agent for

_____(insert name of Principal).

_____
Signature of Health-Care Agent

ACCEPTANCE BY HEALTH-CARE AGENT

A.   This designation shall not become effective unless the patient is unable to participate in treatment decisions.

B.   I shall not exercise powers concerning the Principal's care, custody, and medical treatment that the Principal, if able to participate in the decision, could not have exercised in his or her own behalf.

C.   This designation cannot be used to make a medical treatment decision to withhold or withdraw treatment from a Principal who is pregnant that would result in the pregnant Principal's death.

D.   I shall not receive compensation for the performance of my authority, rights, and responsibilities, but I may be reimbursed for actual and necessary expenses incurred in the performance of my authority, rights, and responsibilities.

E.   I shall act in accordance with the standards of care applicable to fiduciaries when acting for the Principal and shall act consistent with his or her best interests. The known desires of the Principal expressed or evidenced while the Principal is able to participate in medical treatment decisions are presumed to be in his or her best interests.

F.   The Principal may revoke his or her designation at any time or in any manner sufficient to communicate an intent to revoke.

G.   I may revoke my acceptance to the designation at any time and in any manner sufficient to communicate an intent to revoke.

I have read this document carefully, and have personally discussed with the Principal his or her health-care wishes at a time of possible incapacity. I further state that I am at least twenty-one (21) years of age and that I am not a health-care provider, an employee of a health-care provider, the operator of a health-care institution nor an employee of an operator of a health-care institution, the operator of a community care facility, nor an employee of an operator of a community care facility. If called upon and to the best of my ability, I will try to carry out the Principal's wishes as stated or made known to me.

I understand the above conditions and I accept the designation as health-care Agent for

_____(insert name of Principal).

_____
Signature of Health-Care Agent

Alabama	Ala. Code §§ 26-1-2 TO 26-1-2.1
Alaska	Alaska Stat. §§ 13.26.332 to 13.26.358
Arizona	Ariz. Rev. Stat. Ann. §§ 14-5501 to 14-5507
Arkansas	Ark. Code Ann. §§ 28-68-101, 28-68-201 to 28-68-203 and 28-68-301 to 28-68-313
California	Cal. Probate Code §§ 4000 to 4545
Colorado	Colo. Rev. Stat. §§ 15-1-1301 to 15-1-1320, 15-14-501 and 15-14-609
Connecticut	Conn. Gen. Stat. Ann. §§ 45a-562 and 1-42 to 1-56b
Delaware	Del. Code Ann. Tit. 12 §§ 4901-4905
District of Columbia	D.C. Code Ann. §§ 21-2081 to 21-2085 and §§ 21-2101 to 21-2118
Florida	Fla. Stat. Ann. §§ 709.01 to 709.11
Georgia	Ga. Code Ann. §§ 10-6-1 to 10-6-6, 10-6-36, and 10-6-140 to 10-6-142
Hawaii	Haw. Rev. Stat. §§ 551D-1 to 551D-7
Idaho	Idaho Code §§ 15-5-501 to 15-5-507
Illinois	ILCS 45/1-1 to 45/3-4
Indiana	Ind. Code Ann. §§ 30-5-1-1 to 30-5-10-4
Iowa	Iowa Code Ann. §§ 633.B.1 to 633.B.2
Kansas	Kan. Stat. Ann. §§ 58-650-to 58-665
Kentucky	Ky. Rev. Stat. Ann. § 386.093 and 387.500
Louisiana	La. Civ. Code Ann. § 2985-3034
Maine	Me. Rev. Stat. Ann. Tit. 18-A, §§ 5-501 to 5-510
Maryland	Md. Code Ann., Estates and Trusts §§ 13-601-to 13-603
Massachusetts	Mass. Gen. Laws Ann. ch. 201B §§ 1 to 7
Michigan	Mich. Comp. Laws Ann. §§ 700.5501 to 700.5505
Minnesota	Minn. Stat. Ann. §§ 523.01 to 523.24
Mississippi	Miss. Code Ann. §§ 87-3-1 to 87-3-17 and 87-3-101 to 87-3-11

Missouri	Mo. Ann. Stat. §§ 404.700 to 404.737
Montana	Mont. Code Ann. §§ 72-5-501 to 72-5-502 and 72-31-201 to 72-31-238
Nebraska	Neb. Rev. Stat. §§ 30-2664 to 30-2672
New Hampshire	N.H. Rev. Stat. Ann. §§ 506:6 to 506:7
New Jersey	N.J. Stat. Ann. §§ 46:2B-8 to 46:2B-19
New Mexico	N.M. Stat. Ann. §§ 45-5-501 to 45-5-617
New York	N.Y. Gen. Obligations Law §§ 3-501 and 5-1501 to 5-1606
North Carolina	N.C. Gen. Stat. §§ 32A-1 to 32A-14.12
North Dakota	N.D. Cent. Code §§ 30.1-30-01 to 30.1-30-06
Ohio	Ohio Rev. Code Ann. §§ 1337.01 to 1337.10 and §§ 1337.18 to 1337.20
Oklahoma	Okla. Stat. tit. 58, §§ 1071 to 1081
Oregon	Or. Rev. Stat. §§ 127.005 and 127.015
Pennsylvania	20 Pa. Cons. Stat. §§ 5601 to 5609
Rhode Island	R.I. Gen. Laws §§ 34-22-6 and 34-22-6.1
South Carolina	S.C. Code Ann. §§ 62-5-501 to 62-5-504
South Dakota	S.D. Codified Laws Ann. §§ 59-7-1 to 59-7-9
Tennessee	Tenn. Code Ann. §§ 34-6-101 to 34-6-111
Texas	Tex. Probate Code Ann. §§ 481 to 501
Utah	Utah Code Ann. §§ 75-5-501 to 75-5-504
Vermont	Vt. Stat. Ann. tit. 14, §§ 3501 to 3516
Virginia	Va. Code Ann. §§ 11-9.1 to 11-9.7
Washington	Wash. Rev. Code Ann. §§ 11.94.010 to 11.94.900
West Virginia	W. Va. Code §§ 39-4-1 to 39-4-7
Wisconsin	Wis. Stat. Ann. §§ 243.07 to 243.10
Wyoming	Wyo. Stat. §§ 3-5-101 to 3-5-103